Happiness
for
Beginners

Garry Lee Wright

NEWRITE • Chicago

Happiness for Beginners by Garry Lee Wright

Published by
NEWRITE Communications
PO Box 13107
Chicago, IL   60613-0107

COVER: Kelsey Neu Wright

Library of Congress Control Number: 2012904760

ISBN   978-0-615-60790-0

First Paperback Edition

Printed in the UNITED STATES OF AMERICA

Happiness for Beginners

for Laurie

Preface

THE RED SWEATER

When I was in fourth grade I had a red sweater.

If available today, it would come in several styles, sizes to 5XLT, and be described as Persian Sunset or Tomato. But in those primitive days of the early 1960s, everything we had to work with in that part of the spectrum was called "red."

So this is the story of a red sweater, which I wore as often as possible. I loved it because it fit my body exactly. Fit, as in, hid.

I was chubby (also *husky, stout, portly*, see above) and ruddy-complexioned, meaning I blushed when cornered. The sweater was perfect because, young as I was, I had already figured out that the purpose of great-looking clothes is to make the rest of you invisible.

One morning this principle backfired. A mother from down the block stuck her nose (actually her nose, the rest of her face, and most of her body) into the school bus to say something to the driver. It was undoubtedly friendly, probably just a quick hello before her stack of ironing and the latest trouble on *As the World Turns.*

So the conversation had nothing to do with me – except for the last part, which I remember verbatim.

The woman (whom I didn't know and barely recognized) looked down the aisle to acknowledge some of the other kids, then concluded her visit in a voice you could hear over a passing jetliner.

And there's that boy in the red sweater who's always talking.

Ka-boom.

The blow came out of nowhere. Suddenly, the whole world was staring at me. At *me.* I peered around to see if, by chance, there was another boy in a red sweater who happened to be talking.

No such luck.

The school bus took on an eerie, crimson glow. Panic-stricken, I realized it was coming from my face.

There was a pregnant pause.

But no one on the bus gave birth, least of all me.

With no warning or explanation, I had been singled out. I had done *something* wrong, but couldn't think fast enough to figure out exactly what that was.

Somehow this busybody had located my weakest spot and deepest fear: *to be embarrassed.*

(Worse, I didn't realize it was my weakest spot and deepest fear until the insidious woman brought it up. *However had she known?*)

In fiction, or just a world with fewer loose ends, a dramatic climax would come next, a neat resolution that makes us stand up and cheer the hero.

I had several options. First, I could have stuffed the sweater into that woman's big fat mouth, suffocating her on the spot, and making school buses safer for all hypersensitive nine-year-olds.

Or: I could have taken a vow of silence right then and moved to a monastery in medieval Switzerland. Never uttering another word, I would spend my life quietly copying Bibles and helping with the brandy.

But: In the best ending (how I wish I'd thought of this at the time!) I could have

EXPLODED.

The air would rain smoke and sweater fragments, everybody would be really sorry they started the whole thing, and Walter Cronkite would report the first case of spontaneous combustion ever recorded in Northwest Indiana.

That'd teach 'em.

And what an exit.

Any of these scenarios would have made for a thrilling movie. But none of them, in fact, happened.

Instead, all day I relived the assault, trying to identify whatever foolish transgression had brought it on. The sweater seemed to be glowing now, and I was convinced everyone in my class had somehow seen the incident. They were all snickering behind my back, pointing me out as that shameful boy who'd finally been unmasked and brought to justice. *Look, that's him! The School–Bus Talker!*

I imagined being on trial (I watched *Perry Mason* with my mother) in a courtroom packed with disapproving fourth-graders, the unlucky cardigan as my codefendant. Then the bus woman, playing a ruthless prosecuting attorney, badgered me into a tearful confession, which also got the sweater wet.

We were pronounced *guilty* (though I still wasn't sure of exactly what) but I played my own finger-wagging judge. The sentence: solitary confinement.

I incarcerated the sweater in my bottom drawer under a nest of mismatched socks and a pair of summer pajamas I thought were queer.

I also started walking to school, at least until it got really cold.

And that was that.

Traumas and dramas come in all sizes. There would be others not involving wool. But time is an analgesic. Eventually we can look back at something and see what really happened without having our wires crossed by *feeling* it.

Once the sting of immediacy and surprise fades, events may begin to make sense.

Like: Those kids on the bus weren't concerned with me; they were relieved that *they* had become invisible, that the woman hadn't singled *them* out, or picked on *their* favorite sweaters.

Whew. There's nothing like a bullet that misses you and hits someone else.

The driver wasn't staring at me either. He was looking at his watch, thinking: "Sweetheart, if you don't drag your curlers the hell off my bus, I'll never get these little bastards to school. So, *adios!"*

I can even empathize with the mother. She wasn't mean, only lonely, and she just couldn't resist working that captive room. She may have even been *complimenting* me.

"That boy in the red sweater – how does he do it? Always talking! What *stamina."*

Of course none of this occurred to me then and there. Clear perception requires emotional distance. It's hard to be wise while you're still squirming.

The *what* of life is immediate, but the *why* trails along at its own pace.

The following revisits the what of events while trying to nail down the why. It's a look through glasses I wasn't wearing the first time around.

You might call it a *forensic memoir.* There are clues to be considered and a mystery to be solved.

Actually, several.

Like any good investigator, I had to begin by becoming an impartial expert. In this case, an expert on my own life. Everyone should try that once.

I also thought if I could sift through the evidence, I might discover something about happiness.

I'd *heard* of the concept, and often wondered what it felt like. Maybe I could say I'd found some. Or at least had a theory about where the average happiness-seeker might look.

One thing I learned is, you'll never have any without liking yourself.

Which is when I imagined going back to my old bedroom, taking that red sweater out of the drawer, and – with a dramatic flourish – putting it back on.

That felt great, although it was still a little wet from the trial.

Chapter One

SERENDIPITY

Serendipity means "accidental discovery." Most of the important discoveries in my life have come by accident. But I'm convinced there's no such thing as coincidence. All events, big or small, in whatever sequence, are strung together by some mysterious, cosmic thread, often so subtle you can't even spot it squinting.

I consider myself a Chicagoan, although I was born in Wilmington, Delaware, three weeks before the debut of *I Love Lucy*, a show set in New York, where I would live for thirteen years in the 1980s.

That was two decades after the final first-run telecast of *Star Trek,* also produced by Desi and Lucy's studio, a fact I wouldn't have known watching it at Wisconsin State University, where I was waiting to find out if the government would draft me for the war in Vietnam, then being featured on all three broadcast networks.

That was 1969, the year I graduated high school in Chesterton, Indiana, after spending my formative years in front of the TV, overeating as I watched the Cubs lose on Channel 9 and my parents argued in real life.

That summer had been historic. A rock concert in upstate New York drew nearly half a million young people. Two men got out of their rocket ship and walked on the Moon. And back on Earth, I lost my virginity to a girl who confided that all her friends thought I was just too fat.

"I know he's not much to look at," she said she had told them, "but I like him anyway."

She was slightly drunk at the time.

It was right about then, during that ripe summer of '69, that I had an inspiration. I could make all my problems go away by becoming famous.

Famous.

To a seventeen-year-old in a small Midwest town, this seemed like a brainstorm. I had only a vague notion of what fame actually entailed, but I knew it meant financial success, a big obituary in *Time,* and that everyone would want to be my friend, no matter how good-looking they were.

Teenagers also have something inside that has to get out, and notoriety would turn whatever that was into art. I wasn't exactly sure what *art* was either, but I knew it led to celebrity, and celebrities were truly celebrated then. Their lives were significant, they seemed to enjoy themselves, and they were rarely criticized for being bores, boors, or boobs.

I couldn't wait to get started.

Renown looked like a grand slam. It would be the ticket out of my isolated town, unpopular body, bewildered head, and crazy household.

Or rather, *nuclear family.* You could never predict when one of my parents would reach critical mass.

We were dysfunctional long before that term was widely used, and years before the custom itself was fashionable. We were pioneers.

My parents' craziness wasn't really their fault. Some of *their* parents were crazy, and those parents' *parents*, and the parents' parents' *parents*, on and on, back into time. My sister and I still haven't figured out which of our revered ancestors was the first to snap.

But nature makes for nurture, and either way insanity is hereditary. I've been diagnosed with bipolar disorder, chronic anxiety, attention deficit, borderline personality, and post-traumatic stress. Then the guys with the clipboard ran out of space.

(Not to worry. I made progress, and eventually let other people in the waiting room go ahead of me, especially the ones carrying crossbows.)

But like Kurt Vonnegut's Billy Pilgrim, I can still come unstuck in time. So back to serendipity, coincidence, and that vortex summer of 1969.

My Cubs blew a huge, late-season lead to the New York Mets, a team created for displaced fans of the Brooklyn Dodgers and New York Giants, whose "Shot Heard 'Round the World" playoff, I would learn, began *the very same week* I was born.

And ended with THE GIANTS WIN THE PENNANT! THE GIANTS WIN THE PENNANT! screamed over *the very same station* where I worked three decades later.

(Re-cork the champagne. That trip to the show ended *the very same year* – but it was an act of God. The station switched formats to all-religion.)

By then my Cubs had been sold to Tribune Company, operators of WGN Radio, which I had grown up listening to and long dreamed of working at. They finally brought me up in 1998, and didn't reassign my locker until 2006.

By then Tribune had a head start on the latest recession, and was bailed out by cowboy-booted zillionaire Sam Zell, who showed his Midas-touch business acumen by promptly filing bankruptcy.

The Cubs and idyllic Wrigley (the first sports arena named after a company, an innovator in gum) were sold to the Ricketts family, who sold Toyota a sign in left field. I wished Tom luck as he roamed the stands, greeting fans, some of whom asked for autographs as they complained about the pitching.

Change is eternal.

The Cubs and I both play a part, sort of, in the following, along with the the 40th President of the United States, Ronald Reagan, who began his career as a sportscaster on WOC, Davenport, Iowa. Through wire copy, he managed to broadcast Cubs games without actually being at them. I would succeed the Great Communicator at WOC in 1995. Our fortunes diverged right after that.

Mr. Reagan was elected in 1980, the same year I nervously quit radio to try something really scary, standup comedy. That was at Chicago's WXRT, which had made its name playing newcomers like Elvis Costello, who performed an unscheduled song on *Saturday Night Live*, whose first head writer, Michael O'Donoghue, turned me down for a job in 1982. (Analysts say that probably saved the show.)

WXRT would also go on, keeping seminal music alive even after the musicians themselves weren't. Jimi Hendrix and Janis Joplin started that trend in 1970, the year I drew a high number in the Vietnam draft lottery and – no longer needing my college student deferment – took off for California.

There, I first enrolled in a correspondence school to become an announcer/disc jockey, after struggling as a singer/songwriter, right before my big break as a day laborer/short-order cook.

I finished the course back in Chicago, where I was playing open-mike nights in folk clubs and working days at an advertising agency as something called a *media estimator trainee,* a job that doesn't exist now and I couldn't explain even when it did.

My first office included two pastimes I share with Jazz Age wit Dorothy Parker: [1] concocting satire to stave off boredom, and [2] being asked not to display casket ads on my bulletin board.

Ms. Parker partied the 20s away on Long Island, where I would also live, 70 years later, in a world-famous area called *The Hamptons*, which I couldn't have found on a map until we actually moved there.

That glimpse of glitterati climaxed when I lost my job, our house, and most of the family's money in a sequence of events involving a new radio station, an old real-estate deal, and rock legend Billy Joel.

We'll get back to that in a moment.

Those years offered a naïve Indiana kid a rare opportunity to live among genuine celebrities. To study their lifestyles, to sense their hopes and fears, and to realize that sheer luck is often the only difference between appearing in a Blockbuster and working at one.

During my own hiatus from shows occasionally heard by Steven Spielberg's neighbors, I began an aptly named column, *Wright Off the Air*, soon known as *News Junkie*, which won a local press club award, maybe accidentally. It was a humbling moment, and not only because a typo misspelled my name as "Gerry."

The honor came as things were looking bleak, the way distress led to cracking jokes in the first place. A sense of humor, all the experts tell us, is the best coping mechanism around. Funny people are usually recovering from something, often the previous day.

I only wish I'd learned to laugh at *myself* sooner. General Colin Powell suggested: "Avoid having your ego so close to your position that when your position falls, your ego goes with it."

Great advice. Which is why I now spend half my time praying for humility, and the other half praying that I'll need some.

Good advice is always a valuable commodity. In fact, I was once a professional advice distributor, better known as a *consultant*. (That's someone who helps you do your job, right after getting fired from his.)

I also worked as a janitor, and as a door-to-door salesman, and interviewed the vice president of the United States, although not at the same time.

I was a cab driver and a nightclub emcee and an *entrepreneur.* (French for, "My check is no good.")

In other words, getting my story to make sense was like changing a tire with a pair of tweezers.

There weren't many revealing souvenirs of my years on this planet, unless you count three children and a picture of me standing next to Bob Marley.

(And *this planet* is a figure of speech. I don't have anything planned about my years on other planets, although that does sound promising.)

I must have lived through plenty of teachable moments, even if the lessons weren't clear until later. I know I had unbelievable luck, both ways.

Some of my dreams came stupendously true, others just close enough to be a relief they didn't.

So I learned to pick dreams carefully, and to be ready – sometimes on short notice – to give them up to make room for other dreams.

If I stumbled on anything worthwhile, it's that life is a binary system. Things work out or they don't, worry doesn't add much, and the only way to influence the process is simply not giving up.

I read about a strain of lichens that lives under the ice in Antarctica. Exactly *how* is a scientific puzzle, but they hang in there, unseen and unloved, and manage somehow to keep on going. Whatever the biology, a room full of philosophy majors is outweighed by those frozen plants in explaining the Meaning of Life.

Apparently it's to keep sticking around, as long as you can.

Send no money now. We will bill your credit card.

Those microorganisms get something innately that only a chosen few in our own petri dish understand. Those are people who, for whatever reason, get forced to contemplate unsettling alternatives to life, liberty, and the pursuit of happiness. We call them *victims*, unless they prevail, then it's *survivors.*

Survivors come away from their encounters with crooked stories but their priorities straight. Survivors know how to laugh. If it weren't for the cleaning bills and insurance, everybody would want to be one.

But it's an exclusive club, high dues and no walk-ins. Survivors seem to be chosen by whatever authority that runs things to get lost and found first.

Maybe to lead other campers out of the forest when the owls start hooting.

F. Scott Fitzgerald said a first-rate intelligence can hold two opposing ideas at the same time and still be able to function. Survivors know how to function in two competing worlds.

They plan for the best, because that's the way to keep going. But they're ready for whatever comes, because they understand surprises, and would rather sleep with one eye open.

Survivors understand serendipity. They've discovered a lot by accident.

Sometimes during them.

Chapter Two

INDIANA

The beginnings of our lives, wherever they happen to happen, leave a lasting impression, like a beautiful tattoo.

Or one with an ex-girlfriend's name in big letters.

You just can't predict.

I came of age in Chesterton, Indiana. The Hoosier State is rolling and sprawling, with counties in the Eastern Time Zone, the Central Time Zone, and places where locals still argue over daylight savings.

Even *Hoosier* is controversial. It isn't an old Indian word, doesn't stand for anything, and has no verifiable history.

This makes for independent thinkers. Other states split over politics or culture, but people from Indiana can't agree on what their nickname means or what time it is.

Chesterton was a center of conflict in my youth. Five miles south of Lake Michigan and the Indiana Dunes, an hour east of Chicago and several west of Cleveland and Detroit, it was wedged between cities and farmland, stuck between the McCarthy Era and the height of the Cold War. Some communities put on fish fries, mine held an annual panic attack.

Angry billboards went up on the highway leading into town: *GET U.S. OUT OF U.N.* My neighbors thought the United Nations was a Communist front, and getting that down to just twelve letters was the cleverest writing some of them had ever seen.

Another sign demanded, for God's sake, that we *IMPEACH EARL WARREN.* Earl was Chief Justice of the Supreme Court, that black-robed gang of leftists no clear-headed citizen would ever trust with the nation's moral waffle iron. Their latest outrage was questioning the constitutionality of forcing kids to pray in school, my lunchroom's prelude to sinking a straw in the 2¢ carton of milk.

A blackboard in our cafeteria read *God is great / God is good / Now we thank Him / For our food* in ten-inch-high chalk, and we had to chant in unison before we could dig into whatever nutriments the hairnet ladies had steam-tabled up that day.

They wouldn't let us eat until we got it right, which was cruel. But my bigger concern – which no one else seemed to notice – was that *good* and *food* don't actually rhyme.

I became a teenager in 1964, the year after JFK died, when ultraconservative Barry Goldwater lost a landslide election to his successor, Lyndon Johnson, who wound up as the least popular guy in America. But Goldwater was always a hero in Porter County. His campaign slogan, "In Your Heart You Know He's Right," was countered with, "In Your Guts You Know He's Nuts."

But he wasn't alone. One right-wing group, the Minutemen, put up little stickers all over town: *Warning to Traitors – right now the crosshairs may be pointed at the back of your neck!*

One was posted over the urinal at the Standard station out on Highway 20. Things got messy when patrons started looking over their shoulders at the wrong time.

There weren't many spots for teenagers to hang out in a small town (the concept of *mall* wouldn't come along until someone dreamed up the idea of a confined area and guards) so my friends were at that Standard station at all hours, talking music and politics and philosophy and getting laid – which none of us were, so we had plenty of time to talk about politics and philosophy – and we stuck around drinking coffee until the waitress curtly dropped off the check and glared at us to leave.

We fancied ourselves an intellectual oasis. There were a couple underground outposts around, but they were endangered. I frequented one, a used book store that smelled of dust and mildew and was run by a nice man who was an alleged Communist.

There was also a coffee house, Saturday's Child, which booked out-of-town folksingers, served herbal tea, and was run by another nice man, also an alleged Communist.

But those places were exceptions to the prevailing culture. That's why they were underground, and also going under.

There just weren't enough free-thinkers to support anything that evoked Greenwich Village, not in that decade in that town, which was populated by my five friends, two Communists, and three thousand pissed-off Hoosiers who wanted to impeach Earl Warren.

The Summer of Love never played Porter County.

Small towns are great for smaller kids. It's the adolescent years when things begin to fall apart.

My group was too cool for the bowling alley, too old to ride our bikes, and no longer eager to visit the decrepit roller skating arena.

That rink was where boys first held a girl's hand, dragging them precariously around the room and occasionally, romantically, slamming them into a wall. This pre-teen tunnel of love was heated by an old coal furnace, and we'd all come home from an afternoon of youthful courting with an odd residue of black ash around our nostrils.

The elderly proprietors proudly told parents they put extra syrup in the fountain drinks to give them added value. This was generous, but good business. You got thirsty from all that steamy, inter-gender skating, bought one of their extra-value Cokes, then had to wash it down with something else.

Little communities were innocent places then, particularly in the summer. Our back yard faced the Duseldorfs, whose son had once shoved his father, which made neighborhood news. Mr. Duseldorf had boils on his neck, which I found fascinating.

We grew up official Baby Boomers, playing with the dangerous toys that made our generation impervious to fear. We even invented our own toys: break a thermometer in half, play with the mercury.

We lit firecrackers, blasted off rockets, shot toy guns of all kinds. I had a derringer that popped out of my belt buckle and fired *real plastic bullets.*

If you have any fingers left, hold them up.

We staged dirt clod fights. We played Jarts. We rode go-karts without helmets. But my favorite was a chemistry set. You could get by with any experiment, no matter how alarming, because it was an *educational toy.* I swear to God, I used to make nitric acid in the basement.

In the winter we'd ride our sleds. They redesigned the first Flexible Flyers because the runners were pointed.

"Where's Billy?"

"He got nailed to a tree."

"You just left him there?"

"We were cold."

Baby Boomer girls had the Easy Bake Oven. The original was powered by a white-hot light bulb. Little girls loved those. Some still have the blisters.

Boys got wood-burning sets. It's hard to explain those. "They were craft kits. You wrote on wood."

"On wood?"

"The little pencil was heated to *4000 degrees Fahrenheit.*"

And we all loved Play-Doh. It smelled wonderful and said "clean and non-toxic" right on the label. They wanted you to eat it.

One play set even let kids make their own toy soldiers – out of molten metal. (Right, millions of busy twelve-year-olds, holed up in their bedrooms.)

"Timmy, what's that odor?"

"Nothing, Ma. I'm *smelting lead.*"

One scene in the summer pulls all this lurking jeopardy together. Chesterton was still dotted with swampy areas then, and every year they'd hire some guy to stop by with a mosquito fogger, kind of an air compressor attached to a bazooka.

This was like the circus coming to town. The bug-tamer would spray – *whoosh* – and the air would fill with a fluffy white dumpling of toxic pesticide.

The kids loved it. We would play in the cloud.

And the adults didn't say *anything*. That was how people lived then; they trusted the system. The mosquitoes were gone, the vegetation was dead. All forms of life had come to an end. And the kids were dancing in their puffy new funhouse: *la la la la la...*

Baby Boomers take a lot of criticism for our appetites and shortcomings, but remember that we were almost killed by our own toys.

And each other. I was that unpopular combination of good student and bad athlete, the awkward kid no one wants on their team, then makes everyone look bad with his excessively legible homework. *Hey, what are you trying to pull?*

But I was elected president of my sixth-grade class anyway, quite a surprise. Looking back, I realize I was honored with that high office because no one else wanted it.

But it went with being a teacher's pet, my way of compensating for the attention I didn't always get from my distracted parents. I would stay after school, sucking up and hoping for adult praise.

One afternoon I had dusted the erasers, washed the blackboard, and swept the floor twice, and the exasperated teacher said, "Why don't you go *home* now?" (I wasn't offended. She probably didn't want to hang around while I painted the hallway.)

Going to work young also got me out of the house. My first job was a ground-level position. I picked strawberries.

I wasn't really an itinerant farmhand. My friend Dirk's parents had a little field on the outskirts of town. Dirk's father was actually a labor organizer, which seemed very romantic. I don't know what kind of wages he got for the union, but I can tell you it was 10¢ a quart for the strawberries.

Even at that early age, one boy already had an angle. He filled the baskets with dirt and leaves, then topped them off with a layer of berries to look full. Paid and gone before anyone discovered the ruse, it was my first glimpse of the criminal mind. Now I picture white collar scammers as little kids, faking fruit baskets as they dream of bigger things.

By freshman year I was regularly employed at the cheerfully named Barbara's Bakery. Fourteen, and already a workaholic. I went there after school and stayed as late as the 1960s child labor laws allowed, which were open-ended if you could still stand.

Every night we washed the same pots and pans, scraped impacted dough and batter drips off the same grimy floor. If Charles Dickens had grown up in Indiana, this is where he would have worked.

But my world was expanding. One Halloween someone waxed the bakery's windows, and I was sent to scrub it off. Some nosy passerby stopped to give me a smug, misdirected lecture.

"You did it, and now you have to clean it up."

"Sir," I corrected him, "I work here."

(And could have added, "But thanks for the concern, *douche bag*.")

However, I'd already gone far enough. It was the first time I talked back to an adult. I was afraid, but I had truth on my side, and it felt pretty good.

(Addictive, in fact. After my complexion cleared up I made backtalk a career.)

Having mastered frosting spills, I snagged the job that took me through high school and also changed my life. I became a grocery bagger at the Big T.

That is, I *started* at that level, but quickly ascended the corporate ladder to stock boy, then dairy manager, and finally frozen-food czar.

We had a walk-in freezer no normal person would go near. You had to dress for the South Pole, then chop through ice to get at random crates which had been thrown on the floor since Clarence Birdseye was alive. No one knew what was really in there.

But my friend Dirk and I made sense of it all, and were roundly praised by everyone who had the courage to peek in afterwards. It was my first professional success. I wish I'd taken pictures.

Next I even got to be a Big T cashier, a lot of responsibility for someone in his teens. Before UPC codes, you had to punch in prices by hand, calling them out as you went: "Peas, 26 cents. Milk, $1.79." As a result it took about an hour to check out a single Big T customer. It's a wonder more consumers didn't die in line in those days, waiting for someone to call out their pea prices.

But not cigarettes. Everyone knew that those were 12¢ a pack. That generation lit up everywhere. Elevators. Hospital rooms. Oxygen tents. Ads were still all over the TV and radio then, and kids who were surrounded by the tobacco culture wanted in. Adults gave us the next best thing: candy cigarettes.

"You're not old enough to smoke, but you *will* be. Start practicing. The matches will come later."

The Big T meant that after years of temptation, prohibition, and substitution, huge quantities of the real thing were suddenly *right there on the shelves.*

We tried all the brands. My first was Tareyton, which had an activated-charcoal filter and spokespeople with black eyes who'd rather fight than switch. Rich flavor outweighed those injuries.

It wasn't until later, when *our* children started getting hooked, that tobacco companies finally had to explain themselves: "Don't blame us. We only sell our products to adults." That sounded fair.

So at what age do kids become adults?

"I dunno. *Eleven?*"

But aside from tobacco abuse and a few fellows who experimented with alcohol-laden cough syrup in the pharmaceutical aisle, we were an upstanding group of guys. And I was one of the guys.

We had holsters for our price-stampers, just like gunslingers, and talked in slang. If a shelf didn't look full, we would "sunglass" it, the grocery term for pulling cans up front to cover the empty space.

Every job, stock boy to economist, has some inscrutable jargon to make the players feel like insiders. This also keeps the public from finding out what's really going on.

When the store was closed anarchy broke out. We outshouted our best obscenities across the aisles. Emptied boxes landed everywhere. Then we push-kicked them (the "cattle drive") out the back door and into the fiery incinerator. The finale was listening to an aerosol can blow up.

The Big T was my first taste of workplace satisfaction. We made a buck something an hour, the last time I felt overpaid. Between the camaraderie, the growth opportunities, and the exploding cleaning products, it was the best job I ever had.

I met my first girlfriend there, call her Deb. I flirted with her, and she flirted back. I was pretty naïve about the opposite sex, and didn't notice that she flirted with a lot of boys. Given my hormones, it wouldn't have mattered. I fell in love with any female who paid attention, which only seemed fair.

Deb had a trait I haven't run into since or even read about, but I swear it's true. Her voice would drop about two octaves after you-know-what. That was a telltale sign she'd been somewhere besides the library. I realized I wasn't the only boy intimately in love with Deb when I called her one day and another guy (supposedly just an old friend) was visiting. She answered the phone sounding like Morgan Freeman.

Bust-ed.

My psyche may have been slipping at home, but at least one of my personalities felt comfortable at work, amid the puberty, cigarettes, and fish sticks.

Which isn't to say I didn't act out, like wearing a pink shirt with my high school cap and gown. (One kid was in beige, but I think he was colorblind.)

Mostly I rebelled out at the Standard station, getting buzzed on coffee and ideas, trying to picture a world beyond Chesterton.

Michael, Marty, and I were there one night when some rednecks began picking on us, á la the diner scene in *Easy Rider* – Look at Those Dirty Hippies.

I can't explain the *hippie* part. None of us could have grown much of a beard, long hair would have violated the school's strict-as-a-drill-sergeant dress code, and nobody was wearing a flag.

Maybe it was just our aura.

But the murmurs grew louder and louder about those dirty, uncouth *hippies*. Michael was eating a plate of pancakes at the time, and Marty just reached across the table with his bare hand and picked one of them up – syrup, butter, and all – and *stuffed the entire thing into his mouth*.

Michael didn't miss a beat. He just kept on eating, knife, fork and napkin, as if Marty had merely passed the salt.

The rednecks stopped in mid-sentence, four flat tires.

We nonchalantly finished our meals, ignoring the remnants of Michael's pancake as they slid, slowly and quietly, down Marty's chin.

That image is still in my mind. It would have made a great yearbook picture.

I moved away after graduating in the pink shirt. But when I pass through Chesterton I always stop for a root beer at the Port. The car hops seem smarter than we were, and I bet the shop teacher isn't allowed to throw wood at the boys anymore.

I just hope they still get excited about the future, the way we did the last summer I was there.

MOON WALK, 2010
Could they ever pull off something like that today?

"Morning, folks. Help yourself to coffee, decaf's on the right. And you'd better grab one of those little croissant things before I eat them all myself, ha ha. Now, let's say hello to Mr. Butch Baker of NASA, who's stopped by to talk about a project he'd like us to show on our network. Butch, you have the floor."

"Thank you, Les. Ladies and gentlemen, we're about to witness the realization of humanity's most exciting dream! In fact, this may be the biggest–"

"Excuse me, um, Butch. I see here in the outline you plan to stretch this whole land-on-the-Moon thing out for, what, *four days*?"

"Well, yes. That's how long it takes to–"

"We may be in problem territory there. No offense, but the mini-series went out with *Roots.*"

"Not only that, it feels thin. Once they get to the Moon, then what?"

"They... walk!"

"They what?"

"Walk!"

"That's it? *Walk?*"

"Right! Walk on the Moon! It's the single greatest moment in the history of–"

"*Les*, if I could just jump in. Instead of walking, couldn't these guys *wrestle* or something? Fox is killing us with the 18-to-24s. We could sell the whole package to an energy drink, and then viewers could vote on who's the best looking."

"What about it, Butch? Could we tweak it?"

"Well, um, one of our astronauts was talking about hitting a *golf ball*..."

"*Oooh*, wrong sport, Butch. Golf skews a little, well, *old* for us. And the clothes, I mean, c'mon."

"Could he kick a football instead? I'll bet that thing would really travel. Not much crosswind there, right? Put a giant goal post up in some crater."

"Why not *snowboarding*? Mountain Dew would look at it. 'Do the Dew – Cooler than Oxygen!'"

"We should work in some nudity. How about a few babes stow away on the rocket ship, and then they have to take their tops off to get a ride back?"

"You're missing the *big* problem here. These guys are all *unknowns.* Armstrong, Aldrin, and Collins. It sounds like a personal injury law firm."

"That's right, get some *names*. Make it a buddy picture, lots of action. Young guy, hot under the collar, needs a veteran to show him the ropes on the Moon. I'm thinking Johnny Depp and Al Pacino."

"And the third guy who stays on the mother ship keeps cracking jokes over the intercom. I'm hearing Danny DeVito."

"Make it a girl. Ellen DeGeneres."

"Gentleman, what we *need* is a flashy production number. Marching bands spell out 'blast off' in a bunch of different languages, everybody shoots it out with laser guns, and then – right in the middle – up pops Cher!"

"Too old. Make it Lady Gaga."

"Les, this budget's going to *kill* us. Shoot the whole thing at *night?* Imagine the overtime."

"The script needs a major rewrite, too. All this 'foot' stuff. *'Moon walk,' 'small step,' 'giant leap.'* What are we making, a Dr. Scholl's commercial?"

"I'm afraid they're right, Butch. We already have so many things in development, it's just not a fit."

"But–"

"No hard feelings, though."

"Say, Butch, have you thought about pitching this thing to the Golf Channel?"

Chapter Three

GENES

When men tell their stories, their fathers' voices do a lot of the talking. You can substitute "women" and "mothers," but the ventriloquist's gender doesn't matter much. There's still a hand up your back, even if you can't see anyone's lips moving.

We spend the first years of our lives trying to copy our parents, and the next twenty hoping to avoid any similarities. Eventually we see them in context, good and bad, and make peace with that.

Or we just tell anyone who asks that we were shipwrecked at birth and raised by a tribe of natives.

Ah-*ooooo*.

My father had a sense of humor, but you had to dig for it. He appreciated the comedians of his generation, but worked without much laughter his whole life. He taught me to play harmonica, and to understand the blues. This process wasn't entirely musical.

I know surprisingly little about him, given that I lived in his household until I was 17. That's when he left (at the time, frankly, a relief) but that seems inevitable. He and my mother were simply resolving an issue my sister and I had observed for years. They just couldn't stand each other.

He was born Wilbur Gary Wright, in 1915, in Gary, Indiana. Being given the first and last names of one of the Wright Brothers must have been the earliest of many challenges. He was a pilot in his younger years. Maybe that was inevitable too.

What few details I have came from my mother. His own mother died young. He was married before. (I had three half-brothers, and only met one.) His father, in a common phrase then, "beat him with one hand and read the Bible to him with the other." (Gramps was apparently nasty, and ambidextrous.) Dad had been raised as a Nazarene, in a sect that she said made the Amish look like the Marx Brothers.

They even frowned on dancing and playing cards.

This upbringing stuck with my father. He thought the eighth deadly sin was going on vacation.

Both my parents were one of seven siblings, most of them with stories. On my father's side, these often fell into the detective genre.

Uncle Fred was a mythical figure because he died of a heart attack before I was born and I never heard his name except in the past tense.

Another uncle, Floyd, died when I was a child (another heart attack; stress seemed to run in that side of the family) and his widow, Aunt Betty, was always known as Aunt Betty Floyd to distinguish her from my other Aunt Betty, my mother's sister.

That aunt was a WAC (Women's Army Corps) in World War II, and made peanut brittle. Those facts may be unrelated, but her peanut brittle was terrific, and that's the last war everybody agreed on.

A third paternal uncle was presumably alive, but missing. Uncle Dallas had reportedly left his family one day and just disappeared. My sister and I also got the impression that there wasn't an immediate push to drop everything and go out looking for him. So, growing up, his name and bio always ran together – Your Uncle Dallas Who Left His Family One Day and Just Disappeared.

That was one of three things she and I knew about him. The other two: he had fought in the Battle of the Bulge, and he had eaten oatmeal for breakfast *every day of his life.*

Those are the only facts we got from the folks about our Uncle Dallas; they make for a short obit. If there's any conclusion to be drawn, it's that you can have your cholesterol under control and still go off the deep end.

My father's older brother, the only one I knew, sounds like he should have run the government. That was Uncle Sam. But he owned a construction company, also my father's eventual line of work.

Uncle Sam looked a little like Ernest Borgnine, which was odd because my father looked a lot like Andy Griffith. You can't explain genetics.

That brings us to my father's two sisters, my Aunt Lulabelle and my Aunt Lucille. Lucille was usually shortened to "Cille," which my young ears misunderstood as "Seal," meaning I pictured her with a set of flippers, balancing a ball on her nose.

There was a touch of scandal about Aunt Cille – benign now but at the time quite shocking – she never had any children, apparently by choice, which was rare in the 1960s for a married woman, and not at all popular. In fact, there was a lot of talk behind her back. Word was, she made that selfish decision because *she didn't want to ruin her figure.*

Can you imagine? The *nerve.*

So there was an air of mystery surrounding Aunt Cille. Flippers, ball on her nose, and a perfect figure.

I only wish I'd known her as a younger woman.

My other paternal aunt, Aunt Lulabelle, was my and my sister's favorite. One reason was, unlike our other relatives, we almost never saw her. She lived in Kentucky with Uncle Joe, who was a golf pro.

Without quite understanding what this job entailed, I knew it was something special because of the reverent tone everyone used. "She's married to a *golf pro.*" (The way you'd say, "And her husband, you know, *he owns eastern Pennsylvania.*")

Even at that early age, I suspected that *golf pro* and *pro golfer* weren't the same thing. Far as I know, Uncle Joe wasn't a regular on the PGA tour, and he may have given lessons or just stuck around the clubhouse in case someone ran out of tees.

Still, my father and mother both grew up in the Great Depression, so their frame of reference was definitely hardscrabble. Someone who made a living going to work in a Ban-Lon shirt every day was just about as bona fide a success as anyone they knew personally.

As for Aunt Lulabelle, she was big, funny, flamboyant, had a crackling southern accent and – the best thing – *she played the ukulele.*

Yep, the ukulele.

Not one of those kid's toys, either. A big one, the size of a guitar. She could *sing* too, really got into it, all while she kept a King Sano cigarette going.

Unlike my father's other relatives – presumably all crazy, dead, or missing – Lulabelle was just *eccentric.* She mesmerized me. I can still picture her sitting cross-legged on some motel bed, chain-smoking and banging out a showstopper.

(With Uncle Joe, as filmakers say, *out of frame*. Down the hall, teaching another guest how to putt.)

Those trips make for pleasant memories. I wish I could say all my early travels were so much fun. Before the surreal family vacations that would dot the 60s, we moved from place to place a lot when I was little, presaging my own wanderlust as an adult.

I've had 33 different addresses I can actually remember, starting with Seattle, where I went to kindergarten. Before that there was Tennessee, I think, and there must have been at least a brief stopover in Delaware for my birth. Also Alaska (bundle up and stay tuned). I have a map in my head but the push-pins keep falling off.

My mother tried to compensate once by buying me a toy moving truck and some miniature furniture so I could play along. She'd read in a magazine somewhere that this was therapeutic. I certainly liked the truck.

I also appreciated it when, on the first day of first grade, she followed me and my bike to school, making sure I didn't get lost and cross a state line.

We were living in Phoenix then, where my little sister was born. I have a vivid memory of watching out the window on a sunny day as my mother brought Bobbi home from the hospital in a bright yellow taxi. This event was doubly exciting. It was the first time I'd seen a sibling, and the first time I saw a taxi.

Despite being an only child, I don't remember much rivalry. Her head of curly, coal-black hair was fascinating, and I probably welcomed the company.

Our parents seemed to welcome her too, and gave her plenty of the attention we would both later crave. My mother in particular loved Arizona, and later decorated our Indiana basement with a Southwestern motif – lariats on the couch, desert art, potted cactus. She brought in everything but a rattlesnake.

Phoenix was also the happiest time for my father and me. He taught me arithmetic on my little blackboard. We worked together on a Lionel train. He carved a tiny tractor powered by a rubber band.

He joined us in an organization called Indian Guides. It was something like the Cub Scouts, only we all sat around a big circle wearing feathers. Those Southwestern motifs, they were everywhere.

My father would be called a nomad. I only missed being an Air Force brat because he was technically a civilian in his younger years, a pilot working on the DEW Line in northern Alaska.

That was an acronym ("Distant Early Warning") for a row of radar stations installed to spot Russian missiles before they zoomed over the Arctic Circle and vaporized us little Howdy Doody watchers in the lower 48. Fortunately they never did, so we were all safe to go on learning about the real world from a puppet and some guy named Buffalo Bob.

The Cold War made another appearance with my father. As a contractor, he was always surrounded by blueprints. One offered what must have been a fabulous option: a fallout shelter in the basement. *C'mon down, kids! Who wants some canned water?*

Before I was born, my parents were marooned in pre-statehood Alaska for an entire winter, stranded on a nearly unpopulated island. Mom kept a journal of what had obviously been an adventure, including something called a *fish duck.*

After living off the area's seafood for months, they'd hunted some of these birds, and sat down for dinner one night, hungry for a roast-poultry alternative to all those entrees with hooks.

Suddenly, some local burst out laughing at what apparently was a cruel, but favorite, pre-statehood Alaskan practical joke. The fish duck is so named because it's a duck that tastes exactly like fish.

Mom must have told this story a dozen times. Bobbi and I finally realized our parents' icebound winter had been the warmest point of their marriage. We never did figure out what happened between the fish duck and our childhood. (Us?)

My mother's given name was Blanche, but she was always called Sis by her relatives. She grew up in Gary, became a registered nurse, spent 20 years as a homemaker, then went back to nursing, helping to found the Porter County Visiting Nurses Association, the first R.N. to treat patients at home there. She loved being a nurse, and was good at it.

She was a good cook too, another way of taking care of people, and she let me play along in the kitchen with a Betty Crocker cookbook that had enough flour between the pages to be an ingredient.

Her Depression staples were comfort food. Potato soup and lemon pie and bread, lots of bread. She made pancake syrup from scratch.

You'd have to call my mother an extrovert. She was a character to the people who knew her, and probably a lunatic to the strangers she'd strike up conversations with. She talked with precision, like a nurse. You didn't fart, you *expelled flatus.* If you said something was funny, she'd ask, "Funny *ha-ha* or funny *peculiar?*"

Mom was both. She had those dual gifts of a survivor: a heat-seeking-missile sense of humor and the ability to find joy in small delights. Her prized possession was a modest mink stole she only wore if we went out to eat. She kept it in the refrigerator.

She would never throw anything away either, preferring to duct-tape it back together. My sister said she was, in fact, a *preemptive* duct-taper – she couldn't wait to get it on any item that *might* break.

She was at home in the raw outdoors, and went camping for weeks, bringing her portable TV set.

Her philosophy was Hippocratic. If you did no harm, what's the big deal? She was an avid swimmer, and gratefully used a motel's pool when traveling.

Even if she didn't happen to be staying there.

Some families seem to find and marry each other. My mother's six siblings mirrored my father's six.

Her three sisters were rock, paper, and scissors. My aunt of the WACs held down the flank, my sweetest one kept it all in like a blank page, and the third cut people up when they weren't looking.

Her oldest brother was a Gary police detective, a cop who looked exactly like a cop. You always imagined Uncle Bill packing a pair of handcuffs.

When we visited their house I would make a bee-line to three intriguing possessions: an early TV remote (Zenith's "Space Command") a clock which seemed to move its hands in mid-air, and

a slot machine.

That's right, a slot machine. Some uncles show you fishing lures and hunting trophies, but mine brought back memorabilia from vice raids.

People with dangerous lives know the value of a laugh. Uncle Bill liked to play little practical jokes, like sitting at a bar with a novelty-shop puddle of fake vomit in front of him, signaling the bartender over to ask, "Do you (burp) have any ginger ale?"

Uncle Bob was another Gary police officer, a great storyteller who made comical home movies, "homebrew" beer (from his guests' reactions, I gather he hadn't perfected the process) and cracked the first dirty jokes I ever heard. A perfect uncle.

He played the organ – well – and he and Bill were also masters of the accordion. You got as much entertainment as enforcement from those two cops. Lawrence Welk had nothing on my uncles but the Lennon Sisters and a machine that made bubbles.

What were dozens of cousins had their own books to write, and I kept in touch with only one, who took care of me as a baby.

Becky married a Jewish man, the first I ever met. My immediate family was invited to their wedding, fascinating with its Hebrew and the part where they step on the glass. It was an event with otherwise limited attendance because the parish authorities told all her friends that showing up would be a mortal sin.

Faith is a good thing, but religion would be more popular with me if the worst people in the world didn't think that whenever they bow their heads, a red phone rings on God's desk.

Aunts and uncles take on heightened roles in some families, like trading children. Becky would tell you my mother saved her life once.

And when I was sixteen or so, some of my male relatives, maybe after a few homebrews one night, decided to reach out to a young cousin and nephew who seemed to be adrift from his own father.

Taking me aside, very confidentially, they relayed an important tradition about what it means to be a man.

There was a tribal element to the moment, a sense of common genes and shared DNA.

They confided a sacred truth that older members of a clan solemnly pass down to younger ones.

I'll never forget their message.

They told me it was okay to masturbate.

Chapter Four

BOOZE

Human beings have been imbibing alcoholic beverages since at least 10,000 BCE, plenty of time for just about anybody to get lit enough to pick a fight with a wooly mammoth.

That first drink must have been a happy accident. A pile of grain fermented, some guy mixed in water to see what would happen, and the result was historic.

Not only was this stuff *tasty*, there was something about the way it made you *feel*.

That first brewer must have been proud indeed to share it with his neighbors.

"Hey, Grok, check this out."

"Wow."

"Want some more?"

"Maybe just a little."

The word spread. Just about every ancient civilization seems to have uncovered the secret to whipping up a stiff one. Alcohol became an important part of their cultures, for everything from religious ceremonies to medicine to everyday refreshment. It was the biggest thing since fire.

We know the Chinese drank wine since they left behind jars that were used to squeeze the buzzy goodness out of honey and rice. The Egyptians too; they drew pictures of each other tossing back a few. Lugging rocks up pyramids all day can make a man thirsty.

Notably, habitual drunkenness was frowned upon nearly everywhere. That isn't to say a banquet wouldn't offer plenty of the strong stuff, and end up with a few knights under the round table.

But alcohol as a potentially *dangerous* substance was the exception rather than the rule.

That is, until a number of citizens found that they just couldn't stop themselves from overdoing it. These people were roundly shunned as *drunkards*, except by innkeepers, who needed the business.

Today we have a better understanding, and the companies that make alcohol push moderation. But they also have products to sell, so they wind up sending a mixed message, especially to young people.

"Drink responsibly."

Got it. Anything else?

"As often as you can."

And somehow – I don't know when – alcohol became related to sports.

"You like baseball, football?"

"Oh, yeah. Great athletes. Fresh air. Good competition."

"What's the best way to watch a game?"

"I like to get hammered."

When I worked in nightclubs, they were the proud home of the two-drink minimum. That's unique. Comedy is the only art where the audience is supposed to be impaired when the curtain goes up.

You don't see it in other forms of entertainment. "I've got tickets for the opera. Want to go?"

"Sure. Let's stop on the way and knock back a couple six-packs."

(Then you'd have drunks in back of the theater, stumbling around and shouting out their requests. "Hey, sing *Rigoletto*...")

My parents would have started as social drinkers, the way we all do. They were both teenagers when the only constitutional amendment ever to put the kibosh on a previous one went into effect, ending Prohibition, which no one except bootleggers had paid attention to anyway. Almost everyone they knew drank, at least occasionally, and why not? It was fun, festive, relaxing, recreational.

But the forces inside or around a few Americans made booze a dangerous commodity.

Child-rearing is one of those things you can't do properly with too much ethanol in your system. Others are heart surgery and ballet.

Neither of my parents was *a* drunk. To the contrary, they were usually and productively cold sober. That's why it was a surprise, and a problem, when they weren't.

My mother's drinking crept up on me. In Mexico on a typically surreal family holiday, I watched her on the veranda throwing coins to poor kids on the street down below, slurring her words a bit as she practiced her high school Spanish at the top of her lungs. She'd attracted quite a crowd at one point.

You never want to think bad things about your mother, but I finally couldn't escape the obvious. The woman was *borracha*.

Things got out of control after I left for college (I got an uncomfortable call from her boss once) and my 12-year-old sister bore the brunt of her escalating consumption. Once she passed out before making Thanksgiving dinner, and my sibling had to whip it up herself. Luckily, Bobbi's a great cook.

My father's overindulgence was also unexpected. He'd built a profitable company and was always a good provider for his family, a neat trick for someone with only a 7th or 8th grade education. He had a phone in his car and an answering machine in his office, unusual for the early 1960s.

He was successful, respected, and a pillar of our small town's business community. All of which made it surprising when he came unglued.

That happened when I was in high school.

I can see now that his world was coming unglued, and what began as a break from trouble prevented him from fighting, or thinking, his way out of it.

Some business issues were surfacing (he'd overextended himself, I believe, and was also getting stiffed by a big customer) and then some beef with the IRS led to a lien on our house. A self-made man must have found this devastating.

At the time my mother was also trying to find her own center, and decided to go back to nursing – over which they fought bitterly. Another blow to his ego. He came from a generation where a wife who worked meant the husband was somehow deficient.

He lost his nerve, I guess, and started drinking. Or he started drinking, which is when he lost his nerve.

Instead of coming home after work, he began stopping at a bar, pouring it down until he had trouble driving. One night he missed the garage by a foot and sideswiped the house. My bedroom was right above, and the impact woke me up. What was *that?*

His crew repaired the damage the next day. Afterward I tried to fall asleep before I heard his car, maybe the roots of insomnia. Whatever he told the body shop may have involved a deer.

Until those days, my father's excessive drinking was usually limited to off-time with his family (something to ponder) and he brought a halt to my mother's snacks-and-TV "party night" by getting sloppy with Jackie Gleason and the chip dip.

But the *-holic*'s fear and fury were always lurking. As one would expect with a *work*aholic, unexpected things happened on vacation.

Call this *The Tale of the Car Keys.* We were checking into a motel and I was helping bring in the suitcases. I was young, excited, undoubtedly careless. I managed to lock the keys in the trunk.

How, I don't know. I've tried to reconstruct the events many times, the way we retrace our steps when tragedy strikes, like we could prevent disaster retroactively.

But I still can't explain those keys. All I know is how my father looked. The word was *seething*. Rage leaked from his face like battery acid. He could scare the shit out of you without even speaking.

Worst of all, it was a *mistake*. By a kid no less. But he wouldn't let me up. He just kept fuming.

I stood there, mortified, as he *took apart our car* to retrieve the keys. Somehow he removed the back seat and burrowed into the trunk. (Looking back, that was quite a maneuver. Even Ward Cleaver probably couldn't have pulled it off.)

My father never laid a hand on me, then or ever. That's notable, given his temper. I think he was correcting for his own abusive father, to his credit.

But I wish he'd have hit me *that* day; maybe he'd have vented his frustration, forgiven me, and then we both could have hit the motel pool.

But it wasn't to be. He came up with the keys, but he never located his anger.

Or his shame. Strange flashes of insecurity would catch up with him sometimes and cancel out all his success and accomplishments. I got to play along.

Like: One year my friends got busboy jobs at the local dinner house, the Spa. I wanted to, too, but my father said no.

Adamantly.

He envisioned me as a *servant* of some sort, embarrassing him. What if someone *saw his son cleaning tables?*

(There's never any shame in honest work, unless somebody cooks it up for you. Instead I got that job scraping up pie crust. Behind closed doors.)

Luckily there was some final, funny kismet. I was kind of a brain in high school, and some service club (Rotary, Lions, maybe the Raccoon Lodge) had us Poindexter types come to their meetings, get a little award, then give a misty speech about our bright futures – and how inspiring it was to be in the same room with all those Mutual of Omaha agents and Oldsmobile dealers.

The guy who owned the Big T was a member, and he fell over himself to tell everybody that when I wasn't being valedictory, I was in aisle 7.

And all these glamorous young-businessman luncheons – rivaling Miss Teen America pageants in every category but tiaras – were held at... *the Spa!*

For my mother that same restaurant meant a martini before dinner, a glass of Lancer's with, and a brandy Alexander after, her sensible limit. Unlike Dad, she was a happy drinker unless provoked, usually by him.

So thank God I wasn't working there during my turn at the podium. I'd have had to give a speech, break up a fight, and then bring everyone more rolls.

When my parents drank together the Romans' *in vino veritas* was in effect. In wine there is truth.

Extrapolating: too much wine, and then you get too much truth.

Buried issues were exhumed, threats were made. Occasionally they threw furnishings to make a point, but mostly it was just ugly conversation. My sister and I played chess until it blew over.

However, *vacationing* with them was a challenge. I'm reminded of a joke: We took our kids on a getaway weekend. When they came near the room, we said *get away.*

Fortunately, there was also comedy relief. Like when my passive-aggressive father would set off my mother's own hair-trigger temper with some provocative remark, then squash her eruption by

bursting into a song.

You could ask my sister. I recall his repertoire as leaning toward "On Moonlight Bay," but she says it was usually a show tune.

In my mid-30s, I figured out Bobbi and I would be called *ACOAs*, for *Adult Children of Alcoholics.* It would have helped to know sooner, but the concept came out after that wacky movie of our childhood.

AA was founded in the 30s, but it wasn't until 1969 that Margaret Cook's *The Forgotten Children* was published, about chronic drinkers' *kids,* and what it meant to be raised in erratic households.

Then in 1977, a group of Al-Anon members (an AA spinoff for families) got together to compare notes, and found they had something in common beside boozing parents: an alarming pattern of their *own* self-defeating choices and behavior.

There are millions of ACOAs, and children of ACOAs, and so on. It's a pretty big club, but being a member isn't easy to admit. The phone's ringing, but we never think it's for us.

Janet Geringer Woititz's 1982 book, *Adult Children of Alcoholics,* named the ACOA's unique traits. To paraphrase a few, we – I mean, they:

• *Are isolated and afraid of people.*

• *Are frightened by authority figures, angry individuals, and personal criticism.*

• *Become approval seekers and lose their own identities in the process.*

• *Judge themselves harshly and have a very low sense of self-esteem.*

• *Live life from the viewpoint of victims and are attracted by that weakness. They confuse love and pity, and tend to 'love' people they can rescue.*

• *Become addicts, marry them, or find another compulsive personality such as <u>workaholic</u> (my underline) to fulfill their abandonment needs.*

• *Feel guilty when they stand up for themselves instead of giving in.*

• *Act hyper-responsible, and are concerned with others rather than themselves. That way they don't look too closely at their own faults.*

When I first came across this list I was stunned. I had *every single trait*. What are the chances of that happening randomly?

But this roster was (eventually) a relief because it was such a revelation. It put a name to something, explained a pattern. I'd suspected I wasn't right in the head, I just couldn't point to the spot.

I also saw my parents in a different light. Who picks their childhood? Maybe they were only carrying their own parents' suitcases.

I didn't figure this out until later, of course. After I'd started to process reality by spinning it.

I made up stories.

PLYMOUTH ROCK, 1621
How our favorite national holiday got started

"Look, Running Deer is coming! And he seems to be out of breath. Running Deer, what news have you brought?"

"Greetings, Bald Eagle. I – *cough* – have just – *cough, cough* – come from the European visitors and – *cough, cough, cough* – "

"What is the matter with you, Running Deer?"

"My chest is killing me! The medicine man White Rabbit said to inhale the burning leaves of a tobacco plant, but it doesn't seem to be helping."

"Well, sit down and tell the tribe what those trespassers from across the ocean want now."

"I just spoke to Governor Bradford–"

"That shifty-eyed Caucasian! Never trust anyone whose first name is 'Governor.'"

"Standing Bear is too suspicious. These pilgrims want only religious freedom."

"Ha! Do not be taken in by their pious ways, Sitting Duck. Do you forget they promised to do a little fishing, then go back home? Mark my words, we will rue the day that boat showed up."

"So what did they want, Running Deer?"

"To invite us to some sort of dinner."

"What, seriously?"

"They must be up to something. I say we start making arrows."

"Wait. He calls it a 'feast of thanksgiving.' They're so relieved they survived the winter, they're throwing some sort of party."

"I knew it! We'll never get rid of them now."

"Another thing – what are these 'fire sticks' the white people are always shooting off? How can anybody sleep with that racket going on?"

"Get with the 17th century, Limping Beaver! They're called *guns*. And if we had some, we could hunt without throwing rocks at a squirrel's head."

"Whatever. I still say they look dangerous."

"Here's something else. The pilgrims want us to dress up for this dinner."

"Dress up? What does that mean?"

"They're uncomfortable to see us naked. They seem to be a very shame-based people."

"Those prissy pumpkin-washers! They have a lot of nerve telling us what to wear. Have you seen those hats with the buckles?"

"Forget it. I'm not getting a rash from some loincloth just to break bread with those *turistas*."

"I think we should see what they're up to. We'll feed them wild turkeys, and when they get sleepy after dinner, we can go through their pockets."

"White Rabbit is right. Why not have some sport with these squatters? Bake them a mincemeat pie."

"That stuff made from bear grease? Red Fox has a devilish sense humor!"

"Uh, oh – here they come."

"Shhh! Pretend we weren't talking about them."

"Welcome, English invaders!"

"Greetings, heathen savages!"

"We have received your invitation, and will be honored to join your 'thanksgiving' feast."

"That is good. We have more shiny beads to give you, plus some paper from the Great White Father you will enjoy making your names on."

"Our hearts are gladdened. We will show you the lodge where we drink fermented cider and play games of chance. Bring plenty of those beads."

"How about Thursday?"

"We will come in the afternoon."

"May Providence bless our meal and friendship. By the way, do you have more of that 'tobacco?'"

Chapter Five

WISCONSIN

I want to tell you about my spectacular college years. The scholarship, that game with all the touchdowns, the global company I started in my dorm room.

I *want* to.

But my university days ended a couple *summas* short of a full *laude*. In fact they lasted just nine months, almost undetectibly, in a small Wisconsin town halfway between the state capital of Madison and the beer capital of Milwaukee.

That spot had been pockmarked during the Ice Age by kettles and moraines, a good metaphor for my time there. I was cold, riddled with peaks and valleys, and couldn't outrun a glacier.

The rest of the world moved quickly that year. The Beatles ended. *All My Children* began. The first Earth Day and the first female generals happened. Hendrix and Joplin died, both drug-related. The Chicago Seven were found not guilty of conspiring to incite a riot. Mick Jagger was found very guilty of buying some pot. Curt Flood challenged baseball, saying, "I do not believe I am a piece of property." There were passionate, violent demonstrations for and against the war in Vietnam. Defying the odds, I managed to miss most of this.

Instead, I spent two semesters inside my head and out of it, dodging the future, dodging the military, dodging class, dodging the food in the cafeteria. My biggest achievement that year was losing 50 pounds. I lived on Tang.

Like a bus running ahead of schedule, higher education simply showed up at the wrong time for me. It was always assumed I was *college material* (which sounds like you're up for a promotion, as opposed to four more years of homework) but by the end of high school I was living a detective story. I should have adjourned to a quiet room and reread my old Hardy Boys books. The crimes were pretty easy, and the only real mysteries were figuring out *coupe*, *chum*, and why *to-day* had a hyphen.

Instead, I headed for Wisconsin State University at Whitewater, a long-established school in a town somewhat less turbulent than its name. My friend Marty had gone there a year before; I followed him. I had no important academic objectives, or money.

I was experimenting with orphanhood at that point. My father had exited the scene by then, and my overloaded mother had problems of her own. My little sister processed her own stress once by bringing a horse to school.

Like, to class.

So off I went to the Badger State in my circa-1960 Volkswagen Beetle, which still had two gas tanks instead of a fuel gauge. Running low, the engine sputtered and you switched tanks. The lever was next to a hole in the floor, where you saw pavement going by in case the speedometer also failed.

But my bug made it all the way to America's Dairyland, past the Mars Cheese Castle and across the Cheddar Curtain, where Packers fans wear wedge-shaped hats, and margarine was once illegal.

I wasn't in Wisconsin long before my 18th birthday arrived. Meaning I had to drive over to the county seat in order to comply with the latest Selective Service Act – I had to register for the draft.

That law was a bureaucrat's dream, all letters and numbers. The likeliest candidates for a trip to Southeast Asia were classified 1-A. More popular was 4-F, for the physically and mentally unsuitable.

I was probably both, but got categorized 2-S anyway, a college student somewhere in the middle of the line. It was great to meet the people in charge of all this. The woman who signed me up looked like she remembered the war with Spain.

Wisconsin is a wonderful place (I would discover) but my first months there were rough. I spent a lot of time by myself, waiting for my quasi-girlfriend Deb to send me letters, which came on romantic purple stationery but rarely arrived. I assumed she was too busy going out with other boys to write.

I also hated living in a dormitory. You never realize what a private person you are until someone shows up in your bathroom.

The underlying problem was, I was self-conscious and afraid of people. I sat behind two guys in English who always wore sunglasses to class, which I found both annoying and disturbing. I now realize this was because they looked so much cooler.

Joining the hippies on campus seemed sensible. I'd read about hippies and seen them on TV, and now I was finally running into some *right here*. Unfortunately, I didn't have the proper hippie clothes or hair. So I snipped the collar buttons off my button-down shirts to appear more subversive.

I also tried to straighten my curls, thinking they'd look longer. For this I slathered on a thick green gel (called *Dippity Doo*, and I'd rather you didn't repeat that) which produced a hair style resembling melted candle wax.

I even bought a long scarf to look like Bob Dylan on the cover of *Blonde on Blonde*. This was a good try, although I'm taller and wear glasses.

Despite these attempts (or because of them; people probably felt sorry for me) my social whirl began to rotate. A roommate began including me when he headed to the next county to knock back pitchers of Schlitz, one of many in the state where you could then drink legally (and excessively) at 18.

But bingeing on alcohol wasn't really my thing. In fact, the student body split along substance-abuse lines. On one side were the serious drinkers (stereotypically, the guys who lived in fraternity houses) and the other was comprised of recreational drug-takers. These two groups didn't mix much.

Politics also interfered. The stoners were mostly anti-war types, the Greek keg-tappers were more conservative, another reason they didn't get along. It's hard enough to see eye-to-eye on foreign policy if you can't even agree on how to get loaded.

I naturally gravitated toward that first group, the freaks. *Freaks* was a term of pride then, meaning young people happily out of step with the mainstream culture. Not to be confused with the circus freaks who shove things up their noses, although there were similarities.

They were also Marty's circle, and I could relate better to their sensibilities and musical tastes. Plus, by that time I had invested in sandals.

The next step was getting high. I should say, *trying* to get high. For some reason my metabolism and marijuana's storied effects couldn't find each other. I must have smoked a jungle full of Marty's pot before I felt anything unusual.

But he was generous and pot was relatively cheap. A *nickel bag* was a shot glass' worth selling for five dollars. (In 1970 a Brooks Brothers necktie also went for five bucks, but most people I knew tended to choose one or the other.)

The night a cannabis high finally came my way, I was in the sparsely furnished off-campus apartment of a friend of Marty's, passing a pipe and listening to Neil Young. Suddenly my brain left the room.

To where, I didn't know. When that first THC buzz got underway, it made up for the rain delays. I actually started hallucinating.

This was pretty unnerving. I decided I had to be holding on to something tangible to keep from disappearing into another dimension – which seemed entirely possible at that moment. I grabbed a nearby Coca-Cola bottle and squeezed.

Marty says he knew I was stoned when I asked: "Are my dials pupilated?"

Thus began my relationship with a substance it took 30 years to figure out.

But at the time there were lots of pupilated dials, despite the government's new War on Drugs.

Government, in fact, was such an unpopular concept that getting high became a bold political statement, a defiant symbol of generations parting company over the fundamental question of what constitutes reality, and the best way to make it feel like something else.

One of the most memorable photos of the 20th century was taken that year: Richard Nixon meeting Elvis Presley.

For those unfamiliar with that picture or the parties involved, the jowly man on the left with the shifty gaze and five-o'clock shadow was the chief law enforcement officer of the United States. He would soon resign amid allegations that he was actually its chief law*breaker,* and ten of his underlings would serve a total of 20 years in prison.

He, however, was pardoned. Not only for crimes he'd been caught at, but – in a relatively new legal concept – anything we might find out about *later.*

The man on the right, with the hair, had been the world's top entertainer. He now mixed prescription medications to keep his own demons reassured, and liked to unwind by firing a handgun at his TV set.

The King, who collected badges, had a little request for the President, who collected irony. He came to Washington and asked to be deputized as a member *of the Drug Enforcement Administration.*

This moment became the National Archives' most requested photo, and rightfully so. The only thing missing is a Coke bottle in each of their hands.

Another event reflecting the lively times was the debut in quiet Whitewater of an underground newspaper. With the masthead *Good News* (more irony, there was a lot going around) the paper was intended as irreverent and provocative. It was both. This leftist organ premiered with a graphic of the university's beloved mascot, Willie Warhawk, showing off his own organ.

(Even this related to Vietnam. The college's sports teams, ferociously named the *Warhawks,* were once called – get this – the *Quakers.* No one knew who had made that antithetical switch, but most conspiracy theories pointed to the Pentagon.)

Good News was supposed to shake up students and the faculty. For the first issue I submitted, anonymously, a heartfelt essay. The topic was nuclear war.

I was against it.

(You can't say I was afraid to go out on a limb, even if I was putting Dippity Doo on my hair.)

At an open meeting, the editors reviewed my little manuscript: "Who wrote this?" My hand went up, slowly. (I was expecting, "Well, you're an idiot.") Instead, they liked it, and ran it next to a cheerful drawing of a mushroom cloud. My first by-line! And all it took was the end of civilization.

Good News even brought the apocalypse to the school's geography department, which the paper chided as "the home of Mom and apple pie." I was taking a course – required – and the professor huffily held up the paper in class, indignant.

(True, Mom and apple pie aren't big as insults, but he was probably overworked from trying to keep track of all those new African countries, and couldn't pronounce *Zaïre*.)

I slumped down in my chair anyway, hoping he wouldn't associate my name with the muckrakers. I was worried he'd shave my grade, or that the whole department would show up like a flash mob and beat me senseless with an atlas.

I was slightly bruised at that point anyway, skipping some classes (an F in chemistry was my first ever), bluffing through others by constructing dazzling, unintelligible answers to essay questions.

I spent most of my time in my room reading books like *Catch-22* and listening to music, sometimes backwards. (Reversing "Strawberry Fields Forever" provided the *proof* Paul McCartney was secretly dead. This was good for record sales, bad for tone arms.)

I was also continuing to experiment with drugs, sometimes by myself. *Experiment* is a clever word here, since it makes the process sound vaguely scientific, like important research is going on.

And I guess it was. Pot, if I didn't overdo it, seemed to medicate my mood swings (although I wouldn't have grasped what *self-medicating* implied) and didn't realize they were mood swings. I just thought I was creative.

One night Marty and I even took some LSD, a fairly widespread chemical then, fabled for expanding the mind. It turned out mine was big enough already.

Two things about drugs. First, after you introduce something into your body, there's no way of getting it back out. It runs its course, and you have to run along with it.

Second, the desire to escape and the need to control one's environment are mutually exclusive. Choose to enter an alternative consciousness, but good luck in calling the shots after that.

So Marty and I swallowed some sugar cubes or bits of blotter or whatever the packaging was, and the psychedelics soon commenced a-kickin' in. Along with the panoramic effects I'd heard about.

The room started glowing as if someone had accidentally spilled a neon sign on the furniture. Then the music got loud – uncomfortably so – and included some singing monkeys I hadn't noticed before. I had trouble sitting upright on the inflatable chair I was occupying. I think it was a chair.

As you may know, LSD trips are an hours-long (even days-long) proposition, but after 15 minutes inside a kaleidoscope, I started to panic.

"That was fun, *but I need to come down now.*"

Marty just burst out laughing.

Consider yourself warned. There's no off switch.

By second semester I was even more distracted, and running out of money too. I needed a job. And I found one, making pizzas at a local eatery called the Red Lantern. It was a typical college hangout, with one unusual element. During the after-hours rush of hungry drunks, some of the cooks would amuse themselves by seeing how much hot pepper they could pour on a pie before anybody complained.

As I remember, no one did. Wisconsin boys know how to put away the beer, and you could have removed our clientele's kidneys without anesthesia.

But not mine. I was as sensitive as they come, alert to every slight. Authority figures in particular produced a red shift in my vision. This didn't help my career as a *pizzaiolo.*

After some dispute about employee breaks, I distinguished myself *by feuding with the owner's own mother* and trying to organize the kitchen crew into staging a strike. I thought I was Ché Guevara.

And so it was that higher education finally ended for me, some would say just in time. But it took a special occasion, the second draft lottery of the Vietnam War.

I always hated that conflict, but to this day I feel guilty about not serving in it. Three million people my age did, and more than 58,000 didn't come back.

Their motivation was their legacy. They were patriots.

But in 1970 all I knew was that I wasn't ready to join the Army, ours or anyone else's. Some of my peers felt the same way, and the draft lottery was supposed to even things out.

The numbers picked corresponded to birthdays, the lowest ones being the first recipients of a letter from the Defense Department.

The night of the drawing, everyone who was 18 paid attention. This was bigger than Powerball.

Of two roommates in my dorm, one's birthday came up in the high 300s. The other was number two.

That meant Jim would be staying home with his girlfriend and baseball cards, and Joe would be going away to trade shells with the Viet Cong.

Whoever they were.

It was literally the luck of the draw.

My birthday came up 336, meaning I no longer needed my student deferment.

I left college a few months later.

I was finally free to pursue my goals.

Free!

But first, I had to think some up.

Chapter Six

THE SUMMER OF 1970

If there's one dependable principle the universe has hung up with my refrigerator magnets, it's that everything is temporary.

I see the cycles in my life as the hands of a stately clock (another good argument against digital technology) or as two hamsters named Yin and Yang chasing each other around an enormous wheel. I wish I could get those hamsters out of my mind when I'm trying to sleep.

The summer after I left college I was suddenly as driven as I had been adrift. I had inspirations and encounters. It was the summer I imagined myself in show business, the summer I wanted to be black, and the summer I got electrocuted.

Busy, busy.

Change itself was a motif. The gears began to grind when my friends from Chesterton wangled a deal to house-sit on the still-segregated South Side of Chicago, in what was called a "changing" neighborhood. This particular one had been changing from a mostly Caucasian block into one where middle-class families of color lived. By 1970, a house full of white teenagers kind of stuck out.

But our new neighbors were welcoming. And since I'd grown up in white Porter County and hadn't had many conversations with black people (or even seen them up close) this was like meeting someone famous I only knew from sports or music or the news.

Which was pretty exciting. Like several young generations before me, I was beginning to suspect that black people had invented *cool*, something I wanted to find out more about, and get.

I was also learning that African-Americans had invented jazz, blues, and rock 'n' roll. (As a matter of fact, "Rocket 88" by Jackie Brenston and Ike Turner's band was released the same year I was born. Despite what you might hear about "Rock Around the Clock," that earlier, black side was the first rock 'n' roll record.)

I'd also read *Confessions of Nat Turner* and *Black Like Me*, both by white guys, but also *Invisible Man* and *Native Son* and *The Autobiography of Malcolm X,* and Eldridge Cleaver's *Soul on Ice.*

"You're either part of the solution or part of the problem." That made sense to an underdog. These were angry young black men. I wanted to be one too. I already had the angry and young parts down.

In Chicago we met a guy named Jimmy who ran a grocery down the street where I first tasted papaya juice (this seemed very exotic) and Jimmy told me about a clothing store where black guys shopped.

Called Smokey Joe's, it was where I acquired vertical-striped, bell-bottom slacks and a silk shirt. Then I went to a black barber shop where they styled my curly hair into an Afro and even sprayed *AfroSheen* on it, and gave me a pick comb just like the ones black guys used. After all that the only way you could still tell I wasn't actually black was the pink skin, red freckles, blonde hair, and the fact that I looked more like Howdy Doody than anyone else in that neighborhood, papaya juice or not.

But I was beginning to *feel* cool.

Now, all that I needed was a cool career. One possibility related to the house itself, which was usually occupied by the mother of the author Harry Mark Petrakis, with whose son John we had gone to school in Indiana. We were always welcomed at that Petrakis home on Lake Michigan, and John's mother Diana introduced us all to Greek food with her terrific *dolmades* – stuffed grape leaves.

Mr. Petrakis had written *A Dream of Kings*, which was made into a movie. He was the first celebrated person I'd ever met. My favorite part of their home was his study, with its desk that faced a huge picture window looking out over the beach.

I thought: *This is where a* writer *spends his day.*

Mr. Petrakis knew I had creative aspirations and once autographed a book for me, "With best wishes for your own work."

My own work. So far, that was rearranging boxes of Duz. Seeing a different notion over the signature of a man who'd contemplated at a National Book Award was like winning something myself.

That setup by the beach looked pretty good too.

However, authors need something to write *about*. In a rare moment of adolescent lucidity, I realized I hadn't lived long or widely enough. *On the Road* would have to wait until I got past Valparaiso.

But that summer in the other Petrakis house in Chicago, a different sort of public career came over the transom. Less literary (snobs might say less literate) but better suited to the word skills and worldview of an eighteen-year-old.

I decided to become a disc jockey.

This future was based on my past. The radio had always been on in my life. I can remember Peggy Lee singing, "Baubles, Bangles & Beads," making me about four. At seven, it was the Coasters and "Charlie Brown." At 12, those Beatles.

As a teenager, my pocket-size AM transistor radio – in its genuine leatherette case – was always near, and the deejays whose voices came through it were my imaginary friends and real-life heroes. I fell asleep with that transistor next to my ear every night, listening to Top 40 stations from Chicago.

(*Top 40*, by the way, was a format cooked up by accident. Some guy in the jukebox industry noticed the records earning the most pocket change along his route always totalled about forty songs, getting played over and over. That number translated into the countdowns we grew up with. The Silver Dollar Survey was the biggest news of our week.)

Radio, in fact, was the only medium we had. The Internet was still a nascent military plan to keep track of weapons, and TV was still a Madison Avenue plan to keep track of our parents. The top show the year I turned 13 was *Bonanza*.

Even youth-targeted programs like *Hullabaloo* were tricked up in the variety-show style of that era, with dancers gallivanting around in go-go boots – an old person's idea of what a young person would want to watch.

But radio was untouched by square grownup hands. The jocks' patter and antics were a secret code, a lingua franca. Radio was *ours*.

And as I listened to my transistor, I imagined being the guy who said those wacky things, played those hip records, who was having such a blast.

In the summer of 1970, it took only sixty seconds to realize that job I'd dreamed of *could be mine*.

It happened during a commercial for something called the Columbia School of Broadcasting. The leading man was a dashing deejay at his board, headphones in place, talking to sleek microphone. If you still didn't get the idea, there was a big sign: ON THE AIR.

(I wouldn't, by the way, have known that a *board* was what you called the audio console with the dials and switches, or that the one in the commercial probably wasn't connected to anything except the wall. I wouldn't have known that because I was a *civilian* then, which is how people inside show business refer to outsiders. Saying *civilian* makes them feel chosen and special, especially when they're unemployed or bombing.)

That guy in the commercial was definitely no civilian. In fact, he epitomized *star*. He had what everybody would call a *radio voice*. You could also have picked *golden-throated, dulcet, sonorous,* or *bell-shaped.* That voice might have been coming from all the transistors next to all the teenage ears tuned in that night, all across America.

Man, that was fame.

Then that big celebrity turned to the camera – no, that's wrong; he turned *right toward me* – and said: "Does this look good to you?"

I had the telephone in my hand before the commercial was over.

I never waited with more anticipation for a piece of mail. I opened it with my heart racing, careful not to tear the logo. Then I found out Mr. OnTheAir's alma mater was actually *a correspondence course.*

That was how people got into radio? I never would have suspected. You bought a tape recorder, practiced reading scripts, then sent your tapes to some out-of-work – I mean, veteran – announcer who told you how to stop sounding like a kid from the sticks, and modulate like a big-time pro.

They even told you how to *dress*. This place sounded very comprehensive.

I was sold. They set me up with an "audition" over the phone (to hear, I think, that if I had a speech impediment it wasn't too noticeable) and...

I passed! They took my money. I mean admitted me. And get this: their headquarters was in *Hollywood*. I could tour the studio if I could get to California. I was ready to pack.

The Golden State intrigued any Midwestern teenager who listened to Beach Boys records. I was too young to appreciate their musicianship and, never a hot rod buff, barely understood their lyrics. That a "Little Deuce Coupe" was a snazzy car, a "409" snazzier, and a "Shut Down" the worst thing that could happen to either, these were all guesses. "Help Me, Rhonda" I was quicker on.

But I definitely understood *beach*.

An after-school show, *Where the Action Is*, was exactly what California offered someone like me. They made it clear everyone lived on the ocean, surfed all day except when they were taking a break to dance, and got around in sports cars or dune buggies. They were all tan, fit, and good-looking. I figured some of that would have to rub off.

So I saw my future in the land of Gidget and Moondoggie, though my vision was a little cloudy. What would I do while studying to be a famous DJ? Get rich from the songs I'd written in high school? Be a spectacular success as a guitar-playing singer?

That all sounded fine. I wasn't choosy.

The timing was perfect. The summer was about to end, and with it house-sitting season. I had nothing to do but stock up on Coppertone and move.

But before I could, there was a fitting conclusion to that electrifying summer. It even included sparks.

I'd taken a job on the South Side as a night janitor, in a factory where they made dental stuff. I knew that only because there were teeth everywhere.

It was spooky, this empty building where people worked during the day but never appeared when I was around. Like a ghost town where all you saw were places people *used to be* and had to imagine who they were and what they did.

I didn't have much to go on. My only insight into these ghosts' daytime lives was the teeth.

It was like that *Twilight Zone* episode where a man is running around in the middle of a city but can't find anyone. Every place seems uninhabited, then he finds a cigarette smoldering or a record playing or something else that drove him crazy because it seemed like he'd *just missed them.*

(It turns out he *was* going crazy. He was an astronaut in some isolation-booth experiment that unsettled his mind. I watched that show every Friday night. There may be a connection.)

But that's the way this creepy factory felt. Nothing happened after the sun went down except the night I got electrocuted.

That shift started as usual. Empty trash, mop the floors, put down a coat of wax. I was using this big machine you buff industrial tile with. There wasn't much to it for a graduate of Chesterton High School.

Only I was working in shorts and sandals (it was a hot summer and a very hot factory) and I must have wandered into a puddle, because suddenly

ZAP

I was on the floor.

Thus began my own *Twilight Zone* episode.

Another janitor passed through and noticed I was horizontal, then called one of the supervisors, who put down his coffee and decided to drop by and see what was going on.

His arrival made this something of an event. No one on the night shift had seen one there before, and he could have been a leprechaun.

But the attention was logical. Executives checking out are bad enough, but a minimum-wage employee expiring on the clock isn't worth all the paperwork.

So the supervisor, looking worried, kept asking *Are you okay? Do you want to go the hospital?*

I was rocky but conscious, and politely declined. I finally got up before they drew a chalk line.

After the boss saw I wasn't going to enter my next life on his watch, his tune suddenly changed. (He'd been scrambling the jets in his head, working up a potential legal defense. By now he knew things were likely to go his way.)

"Let me get this straight, counselor. You hired this boy to empty garbage, then electrocuted him?"

"Well, yes, your honor, but–"

"Wasn't he working fast enough?"

"For *chrissake,* judge, he was wearing *sandals.*"

"*Ohh*. In that case, bailiff, lock up this beatnik until he gets a haircut."

The upshot was, if I signed a form admitting to inappropriate footwear while being plugged into the nation's power grid (and acknowledging that I hadn't kicked the bucket while operating one) I got to take the rest of the night off.

Had I been killed, I could have gotten the whole week.

WATCH IT, MR. WIZARD!
Today's young people are more careful

"Hi, there, boys and girls! It's me, Mr. Wizard. Your parents remember my show from the 50s, and now I'm back with more swell science adventures. My little helpers, Susie, Billy, and Johnny, are all grown up now, so let's say hello to my new little friends – Madison, Stanislaus, and Ezekiel."

"What's up, Mr. Wizard?"

"Uh oh! Sounds like somebody has the *sniffles*. You know, a junior scientist might find a cure for the common cold someday. Wouldn't that be swell?"

"Actually I think it's a viral infection. But I've been taking megadoses of vitamin C just in case. Too bad they recalled those zinc swabs."

"Want some amoxicillin? It was in my parents' medicine cabinet."

"Thanks. I'm already a little buzzed on Nyquil."

"Kids, today's show is called *Fun with Balloons.* Doesn't that sound nifty?"

"Uh, oh. I hope we won't be releasing those into the atmosphere. Talk about environmental hazards."

"And what if one *explodes?* Shouldn't we be wearing safety goggles?"

"The doctor says I have a latex allergy."

"Relax, kids! I'm demonstrating *static electricity.* Did you know that's the same thing as lightning? It's true! Now, I'll rub it with a piece of flannel..."

"*Flannel?* What's that?"

"Not some genetic *frankenstein fabric*, I hope."

"Or an endangered animal species."

"*Flannel?* Of course not. It's–"

"Radioactive?"

"*Absolutely not!* All right, let's just skip that experiment. Instead, we can use our balloon to make a papier-mâché model of one of the planets, just like in outer space! First, we'll tear this newspaper into strips and dip them in a special paste. And do you know what that paste is? It's flour and water!"

"That's a recycled newspaper, I hope."

"And soy flour. I'm gluten-intolerant."

"*Chlorinated* water? Maybe we should filter it."

"*I'm sure it's all fine*. Next, we'll color it with a *big red crayon.* Did you know Mars is red?"

"Mr. Wizard, shouldn't we indicate where water ice was found near the Martian south pole? Leading to that hypothesis about extraterrestrial life?"

"After that, shouldn't you explain this week's breakthrough on the human genome? There are some troubling ethical questions to be confronted."

"I was going to use iron filings to show how magnets work."

"Gosh, could you just tweet us about that?"

"We have to go over to Madison's house now and put together her particle accelerator."

"Then we're going to clone my uncle."

"Wait! Kids! I was going to make a *volcano* from vinegar and baking soda!"

"*Ooh,* I'd be careful with that, Mr. Wizard."

"Word up. You might want to re-think those goggles."

Chapter Seven

CALIFORNIA

California was destined to be a destination.

Not only for me, but for millions of restless souls who headed west pursuing a magnificent dream that would fill their pockets and enrich their lives. By the 21st century, one of every eight Americans lived in California. Fix the earthquakes and mudslides, and the other seven would be on their way.

The pilgrims came from a thousand places for a thousand reasons. But once they reached the end of the continent, everyone had the same choice.

Put down roots, or start swimming.

So they stayed, and invented Silicon Valley and Disneyland and detectives who didn't wear ties.

Plus, drive-in churches and plastic surgery.

The new Californians came by boat from Asia, by train from Back East, across the plains in some dusty, bumpy stagecoach. After that final leg through the Mojave Desert nursing an air-cooled Volkswagen, I understood the concept.

I drove to L.A. along old Route 66, past two thousand miles of postcard Americana and motels that offered Magic Fingers and free TV. I stayed a month with my Chesterton friend Cliff's family, the only people I knew west of the Mississippi. After that, I was on my own.

On my own.

In the place where Johnny Carson lived. But it was more like the opening of *The Beverly Hillbillies*. Wide-eyed Clampetts, palm-lined boulevard, belt made of rope.

California sunshine greeted me, and there was nothing like it. Bright, yellow, *blinding* sunshine had made Southern California the entertainment capital of the world, the place where nobodies became icons, where you could wear sunglasses year round, even at night, and hope to be mistaken for someone else.

(Movies didn't start in California, of course. The first were shot in New York and New Jersey, then Chicago. But early cameras needed lots of light, outdoor light, so filmmakers made their way to the year-round warmth and sunshine in an enclave of small farms and citrus groves that came to be known as... *Hollywood!*)

The tour will continue in a moment, and next we'll be passing Gloria Swanson's swimming pool.

It was hot when I got there. I saw that everyone actually lived indoors, with the air conditioners blasting. I rented a tiny house a few miles east of L.A. proper right next to a freeway, which seemed like an authentic Southern California location.

This place lacked conventional AC. The arid climate was cooled and humidified by a garden hose which drenched a bale of hay attached to a window fan. The optional accessory was a bath towel to keep the resulting waterfall from overtaking the rug.

I lived on BLTs and apricot nectar. A pound of bulk bacon ends cost almost nothing, which was perfect because that was my budget. Modern nutritionists might disagree, but the apricot nectar seemed like a healthy way to balance all that bacon.

Eventually I became a confused ovo-lacto vegetarian – raw milk cheese and fertile eggs. Not many people stopped by for dinner in those days.

But I fed some anyway. In the want-ads I found a job as a cook, based on my extensive experience making pizzas in college. They didn't ask if, by chance, I had ever tried to talk that kitchen staff into staging a strike, and I forgot to bring it up.

The Steak Corral was exactly what it sounded like. An economy-priced chain, the ambience was as thick as A-1 Sauce. We all wore cowboy hats and bandanas and said, "Howdy, pardner!" to the customers, and there was stuff on the walls to suggest a gunfight might break out at any minute. Only a lack of space prevented them from putting the salad bar inside a Conestoga wagon.

Kids made desserts at their own "sundae bar" (syrup sometimes wound up on the ceiling) and there was even piped-in Western background music, which sounded like someone was trying to organize a square dance in an elevator.

Along with the hats and hankies, we cowhands all wore badges with Old West names. I was dubbed *Gallopin' Garry.* This was a nice touch, although they later misplaced the label-maker and had to start recycling badges. *Claim Jumpin' Carlyle* was actually some new guy named Ricky.

Restaurant jobs seem glamorous in this age of the Food Network, but real kitchen work is hard, hot, and dirty. The Steak Corral was all three. After manning a broiler for eight hours, I had to wash my hair twice just to get all the grease out of it. You could have lubricated a car with the hat.

There wasn't much to the cooking part. Mostly I learned to tell a rare steak from well done by giving it a poke. Well done is firm, rare is squishy.

Squishy also describes my judgment in those days, as when I met, moved in with, and *married* (in a five-minute ceremony across the border in Mexico) a girl I had absolutely nothing in common with, who liked to be called by her nickname, Kitten. That pretty much sums up our relationship.

She and I would go out to the coast at night, and by day drive into the mountains, up the narrow, hairpinning highway until we were above L.A. and could see the layer of smog that lay on the city like a dead body.

A dead body. I was pouring a slug from the office bottle when the telephone jangled in its cradle, and I let the machine make noise while I rolled a fresh Bull Durham and reached for the .38 that held down a stack of bills on my ink blotter like two pounds of heartburn sitting on top of a linguini dinner.

Wait a minute. Wrong book.

Actually, the parts about the smog and the girl were true, and there was a mystery afoot. It was called *The Case of the Discouraged Transplant.*

The broadcasting course felt a long way from an actual career, and the disc jockey portion seemed particularly hokey to a 19-year-old.

One assignment was mimicking a middle-aged announcer as he smoothly introduced Dean Martin records. I pictured them sharing a closet full of velour sweaters.

The Hollywood "studio" was also unimpressive, looking more like a display in a furniture store window. The place was deserted, the microphones didn't seem to be plugged into anything, and the only news bulletin you could imagine being read was that an unidentified perpetrator had wandered in off the street and carried away the couch.

Even brief periods of time seem endless when you're young. Things weren't clicking quickly enough to satisfy my impatience and immaturity. I made a half-hearted attempt to sell my songs, nothing doing. I was running out of lyrics in general.

In short, the California dream eluded me. What had I done by moving two thousand miles so hastily? It wasn't more than a few months before I dragged myself back to the Midwest. Running away from home had worked out like I was six years old and had already eaten up all my jelly sandwiches.

We headed for the North Side of Chicago. I'd lived there briefly as the guest of Marty's brother Charles in the front room of what had been a soy sauce factory. (I raised an eyebrow at the time, but after I got to know Charles this made perfect sense.)

We hit town just in time for winter.

Moving into a spartan apartment next to an El station, we were immediately surrounded by four walls decorated in an unsettling shade of sea green. No one else at the hardware store had apparently wanted this particular hue in their lives, so the landlords bought up the entire lot and painted everything in the building that same queasy color. You expected someone with a ring of keys to come around for lights out.

I found work at a restaurant temp agency run by an ancient man named Busch. His headquarters were in a cramped office that overlooked the Loop, or would have if sunlight had penetrated the windows.

Mr. Busch started in foodservice around the same time as silverware, and he knew every city and suburban restaurateur by name. All phone inquiries were answered by shouting, "I've got just the man!" as he squinted at whatever candidates were dozing in his office to see if any were sober.

The going rate (you paid Busch) was $20 for a busboy job, $30 for a line cook, and $40 for a chef – *cash up front.* Mr. Busch was close to retirement or death, and either way he wasn't going to wait around for someone's check to clear.

I blew through two of his jobs within weeks when my lack of culinary training became obvious. In an establishment where the waiters didn't wear chaps, I was in trouble.

The first was at a past-its-prime Oak Park supper club run by a sullen, boozy chef who was usually half in the bag. You could always tell if someone was making sauce or on it; he kept his cooking wine in the refrigerator.

But I was told the chef represented a step up for this particular dining room. His predecessor was so hapless, instead of Yorkshire pudding (the popover traditionally served with prime rib) that kitchen master plated up the beef with *vanilla* pudding.

You rarely see that on Bobby Flay.

His successor and I divorced shortly into the marriage because I undercooked a chicken, didn't clean some tools right, and gave the piano player a free dinner by mistake. When I left we didn't exchange phone numbers.

The second job I booted was with another high-strung Escoffier, hard to please and also hard of hearing. I nearly went deaf myself LISTENING TO HIM SCREAM but I definitely heard him when he unexpectedly sent me home one day because he didn't like the way I cooked lobster.

That failure remains a puzzle. I can only tell you the lobster looked perfectly fine to me, and I never served it with any kind of pudding.

In any case, it was the first time I'd ever been fired.

And I was devastated. Jettisoned in mid-shift, I had no cab fare, no transit options, and no way to get a ride, so I wound up walking all the way home to the North Side, a trek of some ten or 15 miles.

These dramas played out in January, and the rest of that year accelerated into a blur.

We moved to another low-rent apartment. I gave up cooking and got an office job. Kitten split. I was burglarized by my new neighbors. I moved in with some guys I didn't know to yet another apartment. Then I got involved in another strange romance, and finally, *I went back to California.*

We'll revisit those detours after the room stops spinning.

But for the time being I was chasing waves again, this time thinking I'd make a living playing guitar. (Coming: *The Dilemma of the Drooling Folk Duo.*) That plan, however, proved ambitious.

In fact the quickest paycheck I could locate was as a day laborer, the bluest blue collar position you can find yourself in.

Each morning I went to the hiring place with a hundred other desperate-looking men, nursing coffee and making nervous small talk as we waited for some guy in a clip-on tie to emerge from his trailer and hand out whatever work they had for the day.

It was like *The Grapes of Wrath*. You expected Woody Guthrie to hop off a freight and get in line.

(Temp agencies must be lucrative, by the way. In-a-pinch customers, minimum-wage employees, then pocket the difference. Their profit margin must be up there with pharmaceuticals and the Mafia.)

This company's ironclad rule was, never hit on a client for a permanent job. Unfortunately I couldn't stop myself from violating that one as soon as possible. So when they sent me to some factory to straighten out its cluttered warehouse (shades of the Big T freezer) I talked the foreman into hiring me as something called a *prototype wireman.*

It went well. Pretending to read blueprints, I bolted big cables to other big cables inside a box that looked like an elevator car, but apparently wasn't.

Sometimes a technician would appear, tell us the cables were hooked up wrong, and go away. He didn't seem to mind, and we had no idea what we were doing in the first place, so no one took offense.

A perfect fit, and the pay wasn't bad.

But the biggest takeaway wasn't financial. During lunch that first week a guy came up to me (he was African-American, although that term wasn't much in use yet) and asked why I wasn't eating.

The paychecks hadn't started, I told him, and I was too broke to afford a noontime meal.

On the spot, he offered to share his sandwiches. Just like that. A complete stranger.

I've thought a lot since then about poverty, race, and social issues, but I always go back to that day when a guy who happened to be black shared his food with a white kid who happened to be hungry.

The kindness of strangers. I think somebody put that in a play.

Californians needed all they could get. Still a barely stirred melting pot when I lived there, race played another role in my run of jobs out West. After the factory one dried up I hired on for a second stint at my old homestead, the Steak Corral.

I lived in infamous El Monte, over the complex's carport, which featured hiked suspensions and unusual things hanging from rearview mirrors.

I ate a lot of brown rice and vegetables then, a diet supplemented with daily trips to the Orange Julius. This time I was an assistant manager (at the Steak Corral, not the Orange Julius) but being a restaurant boss instead of a bandana-wearing meat-flipper came with its own set of challenges.

Along with grownup demands I proudly took on, like making bank deposits, there were plenty I could do without, like underpaying all the undocumented workers who made up our staff of bus boys, mostly grown men from Mexico. Some of these guys claimed ten dependants, and I believed them.

I also hired waitresses, not the fantasy job you might imagine. When we interviewed candidates, the unwritten policy was that you added a little code number (on a scale of 1 to 5) to the application to denote how good-looking they were.

It was the most important part of the interview.

But get this: That only meant *white* applicants. You were just supposed to put down "A" for an African-American. Someone decided the clientele wouldn't want black girls carrying their steaks, and that's how they handled it.

So there were really two problems. These young women were secretly cheated out of jobs, and whoever dreamed up this intricate system thought they all looked alike.

Running a Disneyesque eatery presented other twists. One busboy had some intravenous drug habit going, and he came in one night with an awful-looking lump on his arm, kind of a bust for that bring-the-kids-we're-dressed-like-cowboys theme.

He finally stuck on a Band-Aid. That was an anachronism, but a better fit with the fringed vest. The Old West had Calamity Jane and Billy the Kid, but no badges in the back for Crooked-Aim Orlando or Ed the Junkie.

There were so many lawless cowhands behind those swinging doors, we needed our own sheriff. One manager, Don, was from Indonesia and had a multilingual accent which sometimes needed translating. We gave cheap "Indian" headbands to customers' kids. Don always called them "fedders."

We all liked Don, and were disappointed when the general manager, Ron, dropped by unexpectedly one night to audit the cash on hand. He opened the safe, and discovered it was a couple hundred bucks short.

Don promptly admitted filching the money, but insisted it was a short-term loan. He even suggested Ron bore no small responsibility for the situation, because if he hadn't picked *that particular night* to peek in the safe, no one would have been the wiser.

Ron, unfortunately, couldn't follow this logic. He gave Don the boot, wrangler-style, after helping him pronounce *embezzle*.

I was getting ready to ride into the sunset myself. After two visits to that land of golden opportunity, I was still broiling rubber steaks in a plastic hat.

I'd spent my last $100 on a car – yep, a whole car for a hundred bucks – and I was tapped again. But my last manager, Steve, treated me like a younger brother, and even let me stay at his house while I pulled things together to gallop out of town.

More kindness from strangers, and just in time. I was getting by on canned soup, and my shelf in his kitchen looked like an Andy Warhol exhibit.

There were a few laughs. Lacking a bank account, I kept what little cash I had inside a dog-eared copy of John Dos Passos' *The Big Money*. This private joke made me chuckle as I was pulling my last dollar from page 27.

And Steve's house was on a street named Athol, which sounded like you were lisping a dirty word.

So we always enjoyed giving people directions.

Steve's living room floor, like many a bachelor's pad in the 1970s, was covered by a row of albums that stretched to the next room. I remember the Allman Brothers' *Eat a Peach* in particular. It got played a lot and had a peach on the cover.

It also sticks in my mind because Duane Allman died in a motorcycle accident right around then. The morning after that, two waitresses came in crying. They'd just heard the news.

But my bigger shock was seeing them carry on that way. They were too *upset*, too distraught over someone *they didn't even know*, even if they were fans of his.

Their grief was puzzling and troubling, and I just wished they'd stop acting like that.

Yikes.

My only defense is that I couldn't seem to feel things myself. Somewhere during my formative years I'd just started to block out negative events. I stopped processing disappointments.

Which is the real reason I managed to join the Gold Rush (twice) and leave with nary a nugget. Emotions are like radar; mine were disconnected. I'd put a piece of black tape over the dashboard.

So I could never figure out what was going on, going wrong, or going to improve the situation. When trouble said *howdy, pardner!* I bolted for the door.

I was young and foolhardy, with grease in my hair and a lot to learn.

But I'll always be grateful that, once upon a time, I got to do some California dreaming.

I can still picture myself sunburned and nineteen, blowing down the freeway in my hundred-dollar car, palm trees whizzing by, overcome by smog.

Just like a movie.

Chapter Eight

CHICAGO

My 21st birthday came a few weeks before the curious election of 1972.

George McGovern was trying to unseat Richard Nixon, a man so fabulously paranoid that he set the table for his own last meal by dirty-tricking his opponents, even though he was about to win by a landslide anyway.

Then VP candidate Tom Eagleton got drummed off the Democratic ticket after revealing that he had tried shock therapy to treat his depression. The country was mortified. They envisioned him with one hand on the missiles and the other one plugged into a wall socket.

A lot of us thought he got a raw deal, particularly with Nixon in the picture. At least Eagleton admitted his neurons were firing in the wrong order.

It was a great time to turn 21. Meaning it was a great time to pretend to be an adult without having any idea what that actually entails. I was about to meet people with similar outlooks.

Between stints out west I'd fled back to Chicago, returned to bachelorhood, and settled into a garden apartment (a realtor's term for *basement*) a half-mile from Wrigley Field, which in those days was an affordable neighborhood.

So affordable that someone from down the street kicked in a window one day while I was gone and absconded with some valuables, including my guitar.

So I moved another block away and into a four-flat building on Kenmore Avenue with a group of guys my ex-wife had picked up on the El before leaving town, a structure one of my new roommates dubbed the Kenmore Boys Club.

The resident boys were John and Jerry, who owned the place. I was never sure how two 20-somethings had bought an entire apartment building, but as I say, it was an area yet to be discovered.

The *boys* thing was a little misleading, too. Jerry was actually married to a girl, Lynn – they lived on the second floor – but she was gracious enough to act like one of the boys, and we all appreciated it.

John and Jerry were Wisconsin natives of solid Midwest upbringing. Both worked hard at day jobs. John delivered organs (the kind you play, not transplant) and Jerry had something going on in real estate. Lynn was a bookkeeper by day, although it was a full-time job keeping up with the rest of the residents in that testosterone-laden environment.

The phrase *arrested development* has spawned psychological theories and TV shows, but we wore the handcuffs happily. Our developments weren't exactly arrested, they'd just turned themselves in and waived the right to a phone call.

John lived on the first floor with his roommate Les. (Short for *Lester,* although his real name was *Leslie* – always pronounced *LESS-lee*, because saying *LEZ-lee* meant the *female* Leslie, a mistake he found pretty annoying.) A running joke was Les asking John, "Can I use your hair dryer?"

That was funny because the hair dryer was really a motorcycle. Fresh from the shower, a lap around the block kept Lester's pompadour in good form.

He was a man of simple needs and clear-cut goals. Les was slightly overweight, a situation he addressed by drinking nothing at night but grapefruit juice and grain alcohol. He worked days at a small auto parts store, which didn't pay much except at noontime. That was when the owner went to lunch and Les stopped ringing up sales, giving customers a generous discount and keeping the cash for himself.

This worked well until the boss came back early while Les was wrapping up a large transaction, and asked for his resignation.

Les didn't mind. He'd saved his ill-gotten profits and was prepared to spend even more time drinking, partying, and listening to Frank Zappa records.

The iconoclastic, anarchistic Zappa was a hero to all of us. In fact, on the inside of the bathroom door was a life-size poster of Frank. So, sitting naked on the toilet, you would be confronted with Zappa's own image – also sitting naked on the toilet.

Zappa, famously, didn't use drugs. We thought that was remarkable, since we did little else at night, listening to his music and singing along, unless we were taking a break to watch *Night Gallery.*

On weekends we held marathon games of Risk. Sustaining ourselves with shots of peppermint schnapps, the action got competitive, and the dice got sticky.

I moved into the top floor of this over-the-top building. Furnishings came from the Salvation Army resale store. My handsomest purchase was a slightly rickety dining room table, which I made my own by spray-painting it with Rust-O-Leum. Two coats of fire engine red. It definitely made the room.

But most of my time was spent downstairs, with guys who laughed a lot and enjoyed life, something I desperately needed to do. They tried to kid me out of my bouts of despair, which was true friendship.

In return, I gave them ample opportunity for amusement. If I happened to doze off after a long day or a long indulgence, I would snore. Jerry and John dubbed me the Compulsive Communicator, saying I was always trying to get a point across, even asleep.

Like many single men (and, I've heard, women) our housekeeping could get spotty. But we were resourceful. Once, after every pot, pan, dish, cup, glass and article of silverware had been sitting in the kitchen for several weeks and beginning to give off a suspicious odor, we dragged everything into the back yard and sprayed it down with a garden hose.

In short, we carved out a wild and completely unsupervised frat house within walking distance of the National League. The zenith of that year was a huge, building-wide Halloween bash, an event which drew our friends and coworkers, plus a crowd of people none of us knew who just showed up.

Refreshments included a huge bucket of sangria and about a pound of something that wasn't. Guests came as sheiks, harem girls, a vegetable couple – some sweet pea with her tall stalk of asparagus – plus an eminent trio: a monsignor, a cardinal, and the Pope. (They arrived wearing full vestments and even brought a chalice. I only hope some local church wasn't missing their valuables.)

The highest point of my roommates' shenanigans was the night they took some mescaline.

Unwisely, I had a little too. The guys began to kid me, and I started to freak out. I headed out the door and toward refuge at a Golden Nugget down the street. To keep an eye on me they followed – and then this posse saw an irresistible opportunity. They decided to get there before I did.

So when I stumbled in (as they used to say, *tripping my brains out*) my roommates were already sitting at a table, apparition-like, eating waffles.

I was living at the Kenmore Boys Club when I landed my first white-collar job. Pleading *nolo contendere* to dropping out of college, I passed a new metric called a Wunderlich test, and got hired as a trainee at the ad agency Foote, Cone & Belding. (It was *Foote Cone* in ad-speak, which John said sounded like an alternative to shoes.)

I did wear shoes, however, along with off-center outfits a bewildered 21-year-old thought were appropriate office attire. My favorite power suit was a pair of emerald-green, wide-wale corduroy pants with a tie that matched the pants. I looked like an informant for Starsky & Hutch.

Compared to the physical labor I was used to, office work was a paid vacation. Come at nine, leave at five, a full hour for lunch and – I couldn't believe this – *official coffee breaks* morning and afternoon.

It didn't matter that I had only the vaguest idea of what a media estimator trainee was supposed to do, mostly pencilling in forms to be sent upstairs and *keypunched* into the big-as-a-garage, 1972 computer.

I did well, only minor clerical errors. Once I added zeros that turned a couple of thousand into a couple of million, and the rattled buyer stormed up to my desk, sputtering: "What is this???" To which I responded, "Well, it *looks* like a very large number."

(Later I was told she didn't understand my sense of humor.)

Most of my female coworkers did, however. And "female coworkers" meant everyone, as I was the only man in the department. I circulated memos from the Fraternal Order of Male Media Estimators, pleading for people to come to our meetings.

This usually got a laugh. Women generally found me funny. Men would look nervous and back away.

Like most ad people then, I spent many hours in the bar downstairs. The cocktail of choice was something called the Harvey Wallbanger. This was such an ubiquitous drink, it lost its last name about the same time the Watergate Hotel did, and bartenders were simply asked to mix a *Harvey*.

(That breezy shorthand made you feel like a real gray-flannel adman, ready to rub stenographers with Cary Grant in *North by Northwest.*)

I hadn't thought of that cocktail in years until I recently saw, looking lonely in some empty bar, what appeared to be a bottle of Galliano.

Spotting that distinctive obelisk, I asked the server if the bartender could whip up a Harvey Wallbanger ("a what?") which I explained was orange juice and vodka – a Screwdriver – with a splash of that oily, off-yellow liqueur.

She gamely told me she would ask, in the same tone as if I had said, "And instead of fries, could you bring me a live octopus?"

But in a few minutes a Harvey Wallbanger actually appeared – followed by the bartender.

This was apparently such an event he came out to see what was going on. He told me he remembered the Harvey quite well, hadn't served one in a couple of decades, and in fact, my order meant he had to go down to the cellar to get more Galliano. My request finally drained the bottle.

This bar's "cellar," by the way, wouldn't have had a lot of vintage wines or a *sommelier* to describe their subtle noses. More likely my host had to descend into some mildewy basement to locate that cobweb-covered bottle of Galliano between the world's only remaining case of Billy Beer and the decomposing body of someone who had looked like Steve Buscemi.

I was feeling bad putting him through all that, but he was the kind of bartender who knows there's no such thing as a chocolate martini, and he seemed to welcome a chance to show off his mixological skills.

Taking a sip of his well-crafted Harvey after so many years, I suddenly wondered how it became so popular – it tasted exactly like *Aspergum*.

(That was a chewable, pre-Reyes aspirin for children which looked like an orange Chiclet. It tasted terrible, and the only compensation was that once that disagreeable flavor hit your mouth, you knew you weren't going to school anytime soon.)

I bring up the Harvey Wallbanger because it appears in the following, with the only unattached female in my department at Foote, Cone & Belding.

We'll call her Katrina.

She was a dark-haired Greek girl with some vision problem in one eye, meaning the lenses in her glasses didn't quite match. This took some getting used to, but I didn't mind. She was quite attractive, at least to me, even with the asymmetrical eyewear.

I had a crush on Katrina, and would blush every time I saw her in the office, a phenomenon she described as "when you get red in the face."

I pursued her, but she wouldn't go out with me. Finally, after a party at my place one night, she was the sole remaining guest, and she suddenly whispered, "Make love to me." I was so stunned I thought she'd said, "Is there more guacamole?"

Shortly thereafter (following too many Harveys one night) I proposed to her.

And she accepted. I was numb.

That turned out to be the right attitude. Over a long and perplexing weekend, she refused to take my calls. Her sister kept putting me off.

What in the world had happened?

It emerged that she was fighting with her perennial boyfriend, and was just trying to make him jealous.

Dames.

My months at the Kenmore Boys Club ended soon after. Bidding my brothers-in-hijinks *adieu*, I was off to California for that second visit.

And in a symbolic finish (I would soon be back for good, more or less) I almost missed my plane.

My roommates had gotten me to O'Hare just in time for the flight, but too late to check baggage. All my valuable possessions – minus the red table, with which I had grudgingly parted – were stuffed into a large, cheap, newly bought, blue cardboard suitcase.

Now, I was either going to miss it, or the flight.

John had a firm sense of right and wrong, and wasn't easily intimidated. He was convinced that getting my stuff on that plane was the proper thing. He'd also spent enough years traipsing in the North Woods of Wisconsin to be pretty resourceful.

Thirty years before 9/11, security wasn't quite the uncrackable nut it is today. What red tape did exist was no match for a seasoned pathfinder.

Suddenly spotting an unattended skycap cart, John commandeered it without hesitation. And then wheeled my suitcase through the terminal, all the way out the exit door to where the planes were, and nonchalantly *added it to the rest of the baggage.*

Someone in authority finally noticed what was going on, and asked John what the hell he thought he was doing.

A woodsman knows how to face an angry bear, and John didn't budge.

"Sir, I was told that this cart was owned by the City of Chicago. And that I was free to use it – as long as I brought it back in good condition."

Chapter Nine

ON STAGE

The recorded number of actual hermits in the world is small compared to the overall population. From time to time someone is discovered as having hidden out for years in a maze of old *Life* magazines and lots of cats, but not that often.

The rest of us live in society, meaning that show business is the business we're all in. We spend our lives on one stage or another, trying to please a skeptical audience of parents, peers, siblings, teachers, sweethearts, spouses, bosses, employees, customers, cops, judges, doctors, nurses, in-laws, outsiders, busybodies, or just some sleepy payroller at the county clerk's office.

You don't have to get on *Yodeling with the Stars* to understand working a room.

Some of us get to like – and get good at – being the center of attention. The spotlight is risky and nerve-wracking, but the payoff is huge. Who hasn't luxuriated after uncorking a line over dinner or getting through an oral report without blacking out?

It's natural and healthy to enjoy an audience's praise. But a certain percentage of the human race desperately *needs* it, which can get pathological. Some of these people do push-ups at parties, and others become performing artists, i.e., *professional* showoffs. They do what they love, ask that we love them for doing it (and if possible, pay them a lot of money) as they work through their issues in public.

Not bad.

There's a downside of course, for comedians especially. Telling jokes, with so much potential for failure and disgrace, is certainly the most awkward and compulsive performing art. What normal person would want to do that?

The laugh-getter's story is also the most ironic. His craft is usually a reaction to thrills or spills that weren't so funny, at least at the time.

"An unhappy childhood," wrote Stefan Kanfer in *Groucho*, "seems a requisite for humorists, and virtually all who depend on public laughter have drawn on early psychic wounds and deprivations."

True that. There's nothing like a good psychic wound to get the one-liners flowing, and spinning that experience on stage is a way to even things up.

And make art. Re-envisioning the world to reveal its true meaning.

Fred Allen, as big a name in the 30s and 40s as anyone on TMZ today, was deserted by his father and went on to become the sharpest wit around. Like: "A committee is made up of people who individually can do nothing, but together can decide than nothing can be done."

Fred's biographer quoted Seymour and Rhoda Lee Fisher about funnymen and -women, who said that as kids they were "overloaded with responsibility and called upon to be adult beyond their years... expected to care for themselves and act as caretakers for their brothers and sisters. A large proportion began to earn money in their teens (and believe that) virtue is a function of sustaining others.... He or she becomes a public figure who feels constantly motivated to soothe and cheer others with humor, but who simultaneously tells them in a thousand ways that the world is a ridiculous place."

Now we're getting somewhere.

The world *was* a ridiculous place when I was impressionable. And I did become a public figure (at least in my mind) to soothe and cheer others. I was also hoping they'd soothe and cheer me right back.

I began as a fervent little artist, always cartooning and sketching. As a teenager I started fooling around with the guitar and writing songs. This took nerve. The lyrics were heartfelt, but I played as if I had claws instead of fingertips. I didn't sing too well either.

It didn't matter. I was in bliss, adolescent denial. "Hey, everybody, look at me! I'm a *performer*!"

I wrote and wrote, and not just folk music. In high school I concocted a little play, *Johnny Argue*, with a twisted premise: what if the jocks everyone reveres weren't football stars, but people on the *debate* team?

This would be cataclysmic, and I gave myself a part as the befuddled coach – based on our real one, who had mocked my friends for playing tennis, which he apparently thought was unmanly.

The playlet got laughs and applause, and I sprouted a taste for being on stage instantly, and permanently.

It was a taste I'd first acquired during a moment of public entertaining (that is to say, *acting out*) on a fifth-grade afternoon, at a lunch counter and candy store across from my school called, of all things, the Nibble Nook.

Why some retail entity hasn't picked up on this fabulous name, I can't say. But there I was at the Nibble Nook, a shy, socially inept kid – and suddenly I began cracking jokes, spinning around on the stools, and generally going nuts. There, in the middle of the Turkish Taffy, the cheeseburgers, and the RC Cola, I was working the room, and *killing*.

Some girl said, "I've never seen you like this!"

Wait a minute. *I'd* never seen me like this. That was a telling moment. Who was this funny kid? I seemed to be growing a separate personality.

(I told a psychiatrist years later, "I think I have several different people living inside me." To which he replied: "Did one of them bring a checkbook?")

I became George Carlin's class clown. What I lacked in looks and athleticism I made up for cutting up until the teacher got annoyed, then imagining the funny things I would *like* to say flashing on a screen over her head, where the other kids could see them.

I had a pretty active fantasy thing going on.

Which is where performing starts, with an image in your mind that has to come to life. You turn into Geppetto *and* Pinocchio. It gets crowded up there.

I started paying attention to real comedians, and memorized the jokes and sketches I saw on TV. As a safety-patrol boy (all that brown-nosing had paid off) my bandolier-wearing pals and I would usher the little kids across the street as we ran lines from *The Ed Sullivan Show*.

I listened to recorded comedy too, everything from Allan Sherman doing "Hello Muddah, Hello Fadduh" to Tom Lehrer singing "The Vatican Rag."

Somehow I stumbled upon Lenny Bruce while I was still in high school. Probably after hearing a line in one of Simon & Garfunkel's songs: *"I learned the truth from Lenny Bruce."*

Lenny had already been dead two or three years by that time, but I read his autobiography, *How to Talk Dirty and Influence People,* plus another book, *The Essential Lenny Bruce,* which collected some of his monologues. I even did one of his less-obscene routines, "Religions, Inc.," as a speech assignment.

Lenny's angry comedy and fractured life made him the perfect role model for me. He wasn't just entertaining, he was esteemed as an *artist*, a social satirist. He made people laugh – *and* they took him seriously. What a combination.

Lenny Bruce, the original foul-mouthed comedian (speaking from the grave, no less) was the man who led an innocent Hoosier boy into show business. He made me think it was a legitimate aspiration for an illegitimate thinker.

So I practiced the guitar, wrote my songs, and thought that fame would somehow find me. My first professional gig was in 1972 – for 20 bucks – with a partner named Steve Almond, in California. We were a folk duo dubbed *Almond Wright.*

Never big as a musical act, we might have been household names as a candy bar.

Steve and I had been "married" by an agent, Dave K, a big, rumpled, tousled-moustache guy who claimed to have been a studio musician and club sideman for years, playing trumpet. He said he finally gave it up one night when someone requested "My Old Oklahoma Home." He freaked out and became an agent.

Dave dazzled me, although most people would think of the con men in *Huckleberry Finn*, just a fast-talking cat piling one yarn on top of another.

There was one wild story about being flashed by Grace Slick, and one about escaping an unruly concert crowd who thought he was a Beatle.

There was nothing halfway about Dave. He was either a genuine entertainment legend, or completely full of shit.

Despite Dave's best intentions, Almond Wright's career was brief. We rehearsed, awkwardly, fought over song choices, worked up a comedic version of "Rocky Raccoon" (me on a baroque recorder, if you can picture that) but it was never a good match.

Steve was from Hawaii, matinee-handsome, a fair guitarist, and a pretty good singer. Including Hawaii, I was 0 for 4.

But the final dealbreaker was my drooling. Unfortunately, that's not a typo.

In trying to concentrate on my guitar work and singing (simultaneously, which was even harder) I would sometimes lose track of my mouth and drool a little.

Not a *lot*, mind you. If I were part of the Mormon Tabernacle Choir, no one would have noticed. But it kind of stuck out in a group with two people.

And Steve, always the perfectionist, objected.

So Almond Wright disbanded. Another impulsive, star-crossed Hollywood marriage abruptly dissolved, but maybe the first in a puddle of spit.

I went on to somewhat drier evenings as a solo act after I'd made my way back to the Midwest and started writing funny material while looking for paying jobs. Despite being terrified on stage, I was slowly getting better at it.

So far, so good. (We say that right before rear-ending someone at a stoplight.)

One significant evening unfolded north of Chicago, in Evanston. There used to be a spot there called The Spot in Evanston. Those were simpler days.

And my problem was simple. The popular duo of expectation and reality never got together on the same stage with me.

The Spot was technically a *nightclub*, but that term is misleading. You think of a sophisticated, cosmopolitan venue, some *I Love Lucy* episode with Ricky Ricardo at the Tropicana, a big star in a big spotlight backed by a big orchestra in fluffy-sleeved shirts playing maracas. *Ba-Ba-LOOO...*

Nightclub connotes classy entertainment. A tuxedoed maitre d' showing fashionably dressed patrons to their *ringside tables*, intimate settings just large enough for two elegant cocktail glasses and an ashtray.

The Tropicana and The Spot had plenty in common, if you counted the ashtrays.

There was no spotlight, no orchestra, no maracas, no maitre d' (except the guy in a plaid shirt who owned the place) and the stage was whatever part of the room not already taken up by patrons eating ribs, while an overloaded waitress tried not to slosh beer on their intimate ringside tables.

The performer made his way through a set of familiar songs (maybe sneaking in one of his own) while the crowd pumped up the chic atmosphere, which was a blend of shouted conversation, ringing telephones, and people licking barbecue sauce off their hands.

Encore!

And this place was one of the *better* rooms to audition in. Which I did, on an open-mike night.

(*Audition* is a scary and resentment-producing word. *I know I'm good. Why give someone a chance to say otherwise?*)

I would boot many auditions in my performing life, but this one I actually passed, then booted.

A little background.

Chicago in the early 1970s still remembered its first century as a wide-open, gun-packing, frontier-blazing town populated by unhinged pioneers, flamboyant prostitutes, and crooked politicians.

The legendary "smoke-filled room" of deal-making insiders was a suite in a downtown Chicago hotel. This was a city where the fix was in, where one ward-heeler, caught red-handed in some official shenanigan, had casually explained himself by saying, "I *seen* my opportunities, and I took 'em."

Elections were often decided by *ghost voters*, miraculous individuals who were able to make it to the polls and cast their ballots, even though city records showed that they were, in fact, dead.

It was in this environment that I wrote a piece called "Mayor Daley's Talking Blues" (i.e., the *first* Mayor Daley, Richard J., the second one's father) about an imaginary precinct captain on a Chicago election day. The lyrics went something like:

He tried to help, and that's the truth
He even went with me into the voting booth
He said, "Let's keep Chicago clean!"
As he pulled the lever on my machine
For practice we did it again and again
I'm only one man, but I vote for ten

I thought I heard a laugh or two, and there might have even been a smattering of applause amid the smacking lips.

Which must have impressed the owner because he came over and *offered me a paying job.*

Imagine that! (A few bucks and a meal, but still...)

After years of dreaming myself into this moment of success, it seemed I had arrived.

And how did I react to this breakthrough? (Meaning, how crazy was I then?)

I turned him down.

My childhood fantasy of performing in some classy *nightclub* (after which they'd give me a standing ovation and insist I be immediately signed to a major record label) was so ingrained that I couldn't see what I'd accomplished in this much different setting, getting across to that distracted crowd, even scoring a laugh with my little song.

What a mess.

Since that first afternoon at the Nibble Nook, I always thought that I would be happy if only I could *get on stage.* But all I felt now was a vague sense of loss, like something had fallen short.

I missed my own victory that night. And not because my ego was too big for the room.

To the contrary, I was *too* needy, too unsure of myself to hear real applause over the noise of my own inner voice. The one that described life's every defect but neglected to mention the good parts.

We turn now to happy people.

I find myself observing them the way an anthropologist looks at aborigines, studying a culture I wasn't born into. One thing I've noticed, they seem to be especially good at telling the difference between what *should be* and what *is.*

Among happy people, reality and expectation are like two lanes on a highway that run parallel and never get too far from each other.

But among the disgruntled, those lanes are on two different maps. That's why they never seem to get what they want, and never want what they get.

Which is where we came in, with the theory that everyone's in show business in their own way. The only variables are the arena, the script, and how thick the makeup is.

That night at The Spot taught me about its own stage, but also about the other ones we audition on, where reality and expectation have to harmonize.

All performing is an intersection. The momentary, random bridge between whatever you and your boss/audience/pharmacist both need or want right then – and can agree or acquiesce to – with enough can-control/can't-control to keep things hopping.

Acknowledge how *hard* it is to get something across (whatever the message or recipient) and you have to give yourself a point for working up the nerve to leave the house, two for any reaction at all, and three if there's no gunfire.

Anything beyond is gravy, so don't get greedy.

And do your very best to stay loose emotionally. Unforeseen events have a way of superceding whatever perfect opening line you were planning.

Fifteen years after the Spot evening I was at a huge, all-day, mass audition for comics in New York, at a fancy joint in the South Street Seaport. Every aspirant in town was there, the whole future of comedy leaning precariously over the East River.

This event was being judged by three industry power brokers – a club owner, a producer, some major agent – and they all sat in the back row, like the panel from *American Idol.* Everyone in the room knew who they were, and where.

To further elevate the heightened atmosphere, the competition was sponsored by Johnny Walker, which had a little bar going that was busily serving free samples.

I'd put my name on the list, and as the performers before me got up and did their thing, I got closer and closer to my moment on stage.

It was about 11 a.m. I could see I was within an hour or so of doing my set. I was simultaneously looking at the clock, looking at the stage, looking at the list, and looking at those guys in the back row.

Five comics in front of me, then four, then three, then–

As the second guy before me was introduced, there was a change in my field of vision.

Out of the corner of one eye, I saw the men with the juice look at their watches, confer, get up, and walk out the door, disappearing *en masse*, going to lunch.

That was that.

I never saw them again, and they never saw me.

Over the years I got pretty precise in my public figurehood. Routines typed word for word, files to keep track of what went over where, everything memorized, paper-clipped, rehearsed to death.

Some blueprints get so intricate you can't find the door to the building. I finally started putting one last trumps-all reminder on top of the stack.

JUST REMEMBER TO BE FUNNY

After the suits and ties went to lunch that day, I had to do five minutes for the remaining crowd of disappointed comics, who were in various states of shock, anger, or relief at the abrupt departure.

To be honest, they laughed.

Probably because I just wobbled up to the mike and drained the glass of whatever I had in my hand.

"Ya like *scotch*? It's on me."

Chapter Ten

BANDS, CABS & ADS

By the late summer of 1974, Nixon had resigned and was back in California. The country was relieved, although those last few months had made for great TV.

I was back *from* California, for the final time as it turned out, and had resigned myself to sticking around the Midwest for the foreseeable future. At 22, you don't foresee that far.

In Chicago I settled into a charming second-floor walk-up in the city's Old Town neighborhood. Charming because the previous tenant (obviously an artistic type) had converted the only bedroom into a New Age tribute to sun, sky, earth, and water by painting all four walls a different, eye-popping color.

It was a masterpiece. Every night I fell asleep in a black-light poster.

But it went with that neighborhood. Old Town was the city's most bohemian, anchored by North and Wells, whose southwest corner (where a Boston Market now serves homestyle dinners encased in plastic) featured Lum's, serving a highly exotic treat of that era, the hot dog steamed in beer.

A couple doors down was the Crystal Pistol, what used to be called a *clip joint*. A buddy and I wandered in one night, surprised when two women appeared at our table asking to buy them drinks. Even at my most lady-killer delusional, this seemed odd. We left before they could start a meal tab.

Down the block shops sold onyx elephants and incense burners, and there was an edgy tourist draw, Ripley's Believe-It-Or-Not Museum.

Two-headed llamas! People rarely went in sober.

The last and best place on that block was the Pickle Barrel, the kind of bar they still called a *saloon.* You could pick up the underground newspaper, the *Seed* (get it, SEED) and enjoy a frosty mug of draft beer with a handful of peanuts.

And you could throw your shells *on the floor.*

(I used to read Mike Royko in the *Daily News*, and he had a column about this phenomenon. At *his* tavern, if you were rude enough to throw peanut shells on the floor, the owner would come out front yelling and tell you to pick them up.)

Living in those volatile times and surroundings, the only sensible thing to do was to find stability, structure, and realistic goals.

I decided to form a rock band.

This project sounds more glitter-covered than it really was. My ad should have read: *"WANTED – SEVERAL DESPERATE MUSICIANS who won't mind hours of unpaid practice in the basement of some decrepit building as you prop up my shaky singing and mangle my songs. Long hair a plus."*

This particular basement (soon to be our rock 'n' roll rehearsal space) had been an American Legion meeting hall, displaying a sign on one wall with the Pledge of Allegiance. On the others we glued egg cartons and carpet samples, trying to soundproof the place when we cranked up the amps.

One of the guys brought along his friend Ed, who served as our technical director, and was an accomplished geek. Our running joke was to scream at him: *"Ed, the El's broken! Get your pliers!"*

The group had trouble gelling. When rehearsals hit rough spots (maybe halfway through one song) Ed's real contribution came into play. He would pass around a joint the size of a telephone pole. After that, the soundproofing issue was secondary. We couldn't hear each other, and didn't want to.

The band would have other obstacles. One guitar player turned out to be a genuine psycho, yelling nonstop at his beleaguered wife as she gave us a ride to some rehearsal. The poor woman would miss the exit, get off, turn around, get back on, then pass it again. This went on for several round trips, with her dyspeptic husband piling on at increasing volume: *"Recognize this real estate? You've seen it before."*

I don't know how long they'd dated.

Our other guitarist was his diametric yang. He rarely said a word, and may have learned his instrument practicing in a closet.

He played stark still, head down and eyes closed. That was about it for his stage presence. You just couldn't picture him biting the head off a live bat.

Our bassist was serious too. He added several songs to our trunk of delights, which turned out to be even more downtempo and depressing than mine. He said he'd played weddings, but I'm guessing not his original material. The couples would have gotten into counseling right after the honeymoon.

For my part, I couldn't handle electric guitar any better than acoustic. And with my history of ground faults, I was just flirting with fate anyway. So I got a console piano, which looked like I was fronting the Partridge Family.

Our foggy rehearsals and hand-me-that-shoehorn synergy left plenty of time to argue about naming the group. A hung jury, everyone had his own idea. Seeking a diplomatic solution, I anagrammed our initials, which translated to *P.D. Gamet*. This sounded band-like, although you could say the same about C C Sabathia or T.G.I. Friday's.

We never did make it to an actual gig, but the experience *felt* like being in the wings. And at the Chinese restaurant right around the corner, an underemployed musician could still get a bowl of rice and gravy for a quarter. Despite this perk, my colleagues went their separate ways. The carpet samples were left to dampen the rockin' sounds of the next American Legion meeting.

It was just as well. I'd depleted my savings and needed a job. There were plenty I'd tried (a dozen employers so far, one for every two years of life) and a famous line of work I hadn't sampled yet.

I decided to become a cab driver.

The taxi companies were always hiring; every unmanned vehicle, no matter how dilapidated, was an opening. I needed only a chauffeur's license.

You've seen those. It's that laminated mug shot of the guy talking on his cellphone in the front seat while neighboring drivers rediscover their brakes and you vibrate in back, rediscovering God.

It's posted next to an incoherent fare schedule, along with things the driver isn't allowed to get by with, no matter how many children he's supporting. Plus, directions for filing a complaint, if you have any energy left after jumping from a moving vehicle.

In my day you had to get fingerprinted (a cheery touch) and then take a goofy geography test: "What's at 1060 W. Addison?" (It's Wrigley Field, but you might be better off cruising the North Side, looking for a big green building.)

The cab company provided training, which turned out to be one afternoon riding around with a jaded veteran driver who elaborated on what a prick the taxi commissioner was, then recommended we handle complainers by telling them to fuck off. "They can go stand up on the *long white cab*."

Thus legally licensed and professionally schooled, I reported to the company's garage, where I was assigned an ancient, beat-up vehicle by a guy who looked like he'd been fingerprinted more than once.

I was officially a cab driver.

Free-spirit jobs can mean working for free if you're not careful. The taxi business taught me the value of money by deconstructing it. From dead zero every morning, I had to yield enough to feed, clothe, and house myself. I once wrote a story, "A Dime At a Time," about watching the meter click – oh, so slowly – at each 10-cent notch.

An entire 12-hour shift might net fifty bucks after gas and cab rental, called the daily *nut*, or overhead.

(*Nut*, by the way, seems to date from the 19th century, when the local sheriff would remove some actual, essential nut from the circus's machinery, holding it as a deposit until the troupe settled their affairs properly before skedaddling out of town. Times have changed, but the authorities still have a system to hang on to cab drivers' essential nuts.)

Taxis were radio-dispatched when I drove. The speaker would crackle: "21, at the post." If you were first in line at the Clark/Fullerton cab stand, someone close needed a ride. You were free to make a blind auction bid followed by a poker bluff.

You had maybe two seconds to grab the mike, announce your cab number, then release the button in time to hear the whole address, trying to write it down while wondering if he'd said "Halsted" or "Altgeld."

Twenty tense minutes passed as you raced to get there before the customer called back to complain, including time to figure out where *there* was. You might have to pull out a map or street guide, or just floor it in some likely direction until the dispatcher called back annoyed or you started seeing boats.

You were supposed to go wherever riders wanted (a legal right) but hoped that didn't include so-called *bad neighborhoods,* where you'd get stolen from, stranded, stiffed, or shot.

You were also responsible for any damage to your vehicle. Mine turned out to be slightly wider than an alley I turned into looking for a shortcut one day.

Robert DeNiro's taxi driver, with the Mohawk and firearms, is a popular image of the unbalanced chauffeur who relaxes by planning assassinations. But I found most of the abnormal psychology coming from the other side of the plexiglass.

Traffic seemed to be a puzzling concept. I needed that reminder from the kid's Batman costume. *Warning: Cape does not allow user to fly.*

Customers could be rude, or just condescending. One complimented my fluent English.

A Gold Coast matron, undertipping me as I delivered her many packages safely home, sighed to her doorman (in the tone you'd use after birthing quintuplets) "What an awful day I had *shopping!*"

She should have tried mine. One long airport trip was rung up by a remarkably unappealing woman who offered to trade a *you-know-what* for the fare.

(Not to be a prude, but this was at *9 o'clock in the morning.* Apparently she didn't carry a lot of cash.)

By the time I started keeping a tire iron under my front seat, I realized I'd grown impatient with the cab-riding public. I was my own boss, but both of us were going broke. Forced to re-don the harness of a straight job and its regular paycheck, I had my four ties dry-cleaned and went back to advertising.

The firm was on the banks of the Chicago River, right in the stunning Wrigley Building. Erected in the 1920s, walking into that architectural wonder felt like going to work with Ben Hecht.

There were even uniformed elevator operators still on duty, although everything was automated by that time, and those elderly men at the end of their grandfathered union contract had nothing much to do but ride up and down all day and try not to look hurt when people pressed their own buttons.

My new/old office was next to an iron-worked stairwell in the back, with just enough room for a desk. This one was already covered by an avalanche of paper. Whomever I replaced had left in a hurry, possibly swallowing something on the way out.

My first assignment was to burrow through this haystack, all dunning notices from TV stations that had run commercials on our clients' behalf with no record on our end of anyone having asked them to.

This was daunting at first. But I soon saw my situation was win-win. Since no one had been able to make sense of this landfill, the worst I could do was rearrange the pile. So I did, in alphabetical order, chronological order, and then ascending order based on how many threats were with the invoices.

This must have done the trick, since I was soon promoted to assistant buyer. I was always at my best in a job where I had no idea what I was doing.

My social-cue equipment was still warming up in those days, and navigating coworkers could be tricky. As at Foote, Cone, men were the minority.

In fact, I was one of just two male employees, the other being a secretary (an uncommon job for men, even after the preferred nomenclature changed to *administrative assistant*) but he had been a clerk for General Westmoreland in the Vietnam-era army, so that settled that.

We hardly knew each other, but every morning he appeared at my desk, without warning or context, and launched into a *furious* tirade about a sporting event from the day before. He was always highly agitated about some blown call, lopsided score, or ill-advised trade.

I couldn't keep up with this fire-breathing fan. But I would nod in vigorous agreement anyway, laying it on especially thick when I couldn't figure out who had dropped the ball he was so livid about, or even what kind of ball it was.

Then I saw our purpose in each other's lives.

These rants were simply one outnumbered man's way of marking his masculinity in that all-female environment. If the only thing I had in common with this athletic supporter was the need for one, that feature was in short supply there. And he just wasn't comfortable going off on the infield fly rule in front of women.

We bonded after that, and I imagined us knocking back Old Styles together as he typed my letters.

The most illuminating lessons from that corner of the business world were about power. One buyer (the misogynistic term was *media queen*) got off by grinding the reps who called on her. This executive, who chewed gum with her mouth open, owned just two dresses (brown and black) which she wore on alternating days without having them visibly cleaned.

To deal with her required manners and grooming, and you had to bring both.

These women, I was told, treated attention from TV salesmen – mostly well-appointed young men – as a substitute for sex. You'd have to say there were some kinky elements to their account management.

Like: it was (probably) a joke, but the two-dress buyer actually had a kneeler in her office. A *kneeler*, like in a Catholic church. And (I wish I were making this up) I personally witnessed a couple of them trying to amuse her with *hand puppets*.

Don't ever be surprised by what people will do for money, particularly if the alternative is even more horrifying.

(See "substitute for," above.)

My bosses were Dick and Norma, surrogate parents to the much younger staff. We didn't care that they drank their noontime meal. The multiple-martini lunch was still in full splash, and this, after all, was *advertising*. They were cold sober in the morning, good businesspeople, and nice to me. Norma only yelled at reps, and Dick only yelled at Norma.

The job they gave me was important – spending other people's money usually is. I also did projects for them that propped up my self-confidence.

One was a little station outside Bowling Green, Kentucky, which we never bought because they were a little station outside of Bowling Green, Kentucky. But they complained to our client, who complained to us. I was given the labyrinthine task of proving them the smallest of potatoes.

And what a job I did! Like a forensic accountant for the Treasury Department, I went to work *exposing* them. My final report was a tapestry of statistics, equations, and even a color-coded map, which I drew with crayons.

Except for the boozy afternoons, it was like being in grade school again.

I could, and probably should, have stayed in this cozy womb a little longer. But I was a restless youth.

They say compulsive gamblers aren't anxious for money, but for *action.* My constant itch was to climb another notch, to seek out the next experience.

The ones that year had all been enlightening. Now I could understand how the Beatles came to break up, why I felt compelled to overtip cab drivers even more if they got lost, and what unspeakable acts may have been necessary to put Spray 'n Wash on *Good Morning America.*

But the next stop was a real surprise.

Chapter Eleven

FINE ROCK

A coffee shop a few blocks away has a big, hand-lettered sign in its window:

3 FRIED EGGS, $2.99

This seems straightforward enough, unless you're stopped at a light long enough to start thinking about it. Like, is there a surcharge for *scrambling*?

"Sorry, pal. We're out of business if we break out the whisk for every joker that comes in here."

Maybe the cook's just touchy. "That's right, *FRIED*. So don't mention soft-boiled or some crazy omelet. And don't even *think* about poached."

Or this is a closeout special for three specific eggs.

"Somebody sent 'em back, but they're still good. The sale ends Monday."

The ad I answered in the spring of 1975 also left a few points open to interpretation. Its key words – *sales, radio,* and *night* – were plain enough, but the combination could be read as if business would only be conducted under the cover of darkness.

That turned out not to be the case, but close. The selling would go on during the day. It was the radio station that only happened at night.

I'd never heard of this. I would soon learn that neither had anyone else, except for a select few who knew WXRT was a new, semi-experimental, quasi-underground "progressive rock" station dreamed up by three young guys, one of whom took my call.

Good start. At least they had telephones.

That's more than I could say. Not wanting to nose around for a new job from my old office (this was twenty years before cellular convenience) I would sneak down to the subway pay phone with a pocketful of quarters and try to get in a quick conversation between the "A" and "B" trains.

Seth invited me to the station, which turned out to be a one-story, cinder-block, *bunker* of a building on the Northwest Side, distinguished only by a huge antenna that loomed tall over that otherwise unassuming neighborhood. Without the tower, it could have been any shop or warehouse.

In other words, nothing about the place said *SHOW BUSINESS.* No red carpet, no fans pressing against any velvet ropes, and the only bright lights were over at the used-car lot on Cicero.

Seth himself let me in. It was after hours, and a radio station with nobody around can be as spooky as that factory where they made teeth. Deserted hallways led to his office, which looked like a grad student's hideaway. If you were running an underground radio station and didn't want anybody to find out, this was where you'd be.

At an old wooden teacher's desk, Seth explained that they broadcast on a frequency usually devoted to brokered foreign-language programs.

I recognized *foreign* and *language,* but *brokered* was a new term.

It meant buying a block of air time, putting on a niche-targeted show, then re-selling the time to businesses in that community. Given this labor-intensive setup and the modest individual audiences ("Welcome to the Lithuanian Hour!") you don't see much brokered radio now.

You didn't see a lot then.

But neither did you see – or hear – anything that sounded like free-form radio coming from a serious commercial station. There were three choices for music devotees. 1) narrow, "all hit" stations; 2) self-conscious college deejays trying to be obscure; or 3) shut up and buy your own records.

"Alternative" stations were around, but beaming across the street, not the city, and tended to be inaccessible. Most of them presented an alternative to something you'd actually want to listen to.

But at WXRT, along came business manager Seth, program director John, and music director Bob, who convinced the station's owner, Dan, to give some concept called *progressive rock* a shot after the Lithuanians had gone home for the day.

When I showed up there in 1975, the music was coming on at 10 p.m. and holding forth through the overnight hours until it finally made room for a Spanish-language show when the sun came up.

This transition must have been a little abrupt for both the early-rising Hispanic community and WXRT's core audience of late-to-bed partiers.

"Want another one?"

"Nah, I don't think so, man. Hey, were the last eight records all Santana?"

XRT was all over the spectrum in those days, playing real folk, jazz, blues, and even classical in addition to all permutations of rock. The music library filled a room. The format was supposed to sound like there wasn't any format.

The station's eclectic mix and cult vibe was already attracting devoted listeners and a reputation as the avant-garde, undiscovered spot on the dial. Its laid-back jocks were musicologists who played "deep" cuts from important bands as well as new, under-the-radar artists no one else would touch. Many unknowns WXRT got behind in the 70s became superstars. Springsteen, U2, dozens more.

There were also some clunkers, which is why being cutting edge isn't always commercial. Some wit said: "XRT plays the music you want to hear, before you want to hear it."

A few of the segues from Chopin to David Bowie were a little jarring too.

But I still thought I could sell this hip idea to sponsors – even though my only previous sales experience was a mercifully short week in college (before the pizza place) selling kitchen cutlery door-to-door.

Ding-DONG.

Now *that* was a job. As the Fuller Brush Man and Willy Loman, I had a sales manager who blended Alec Baldwin's character in *Glengarry Glen Ross* with Neidermeyer in *Animal House*.

Sales training resembled a Nuremberg rally. Only the big swastika flags were missing. We were browbeaten and brainwashed. *This kitchenware is a thing of destiny.* IT ACTUALLY SELLS ITSELF!

There were a few protocols. You were supposed to greet any woman who answered the door as "Mom." (This must have been confusing for some of the area's elderly female residents.)

But once inside, you simply emptied your sample case – *with a dramatic flourish* – on her dining room table. How could she possibly say no to that shiny new kitchenware?

She would knock you over reaching for her checkbook.

The actuality was a little different.

What country cook needs all that stuff? There were no takers. The job mostly entailed touring rural Wisconsin, rousting some poor farmer's wife and asking: "Hi! Want to see my knives?"

I retired before somebody called the state police.

Fortunately, the only sharp objects at WXRT were the needles on the turntables, and Seth hired me. As business manager, he'd been doing all the deals, so that technically made me the station's first salesperson. Someday there will be a plaque.

I took to the task like an evangelist. It was my *own personal mission* to put the station across. Everyone who worked there felt that way. Not only were we trying to pay the rent on our own terms, we were the stewards of rock music and the counterculture that represented. It was Woodstock with briefcases.

There were obstacles. One was our part-time status. The first thing you tried with a retailer was to get him to play us in his store, thus vesting him in our camp and hopefully boosting the listenership.

But more than once someone finally changed the dial, only to open the next morning and hear

¡Buenos días, amigos!

Some of those deals fell through. They probably thought we wanted them to sponsor bullfights.

WXRT's target was also on the cusp of change. Older Baby Boomers were hitting their thirties then, time to see whether hippies would become yuppies, with real disposable incomes, or just better dope.

"Mr. Pennybags, I'm asking you to join our growing list of advertisers."

"The waterbed dealer and army surplus store?"

"Right. But remember, our audience is evolving."

"What do they have that they didn't last month?"

"Jobs."

WXRT's critics said our typical listener tossed his couch cushions for cigarette money. We had to prove he could afford a whole new couch. Winning the argument often enough to keep the doors open, the station was on its way.

Me, too.

My boss was a few years older, a mentor who took a chance on an unsophisticated youngster, then steered the befuddled lad through a complex universe of concert promoters, record labels, and any products which might be of interest to the microcosm that knew who the Talking Heads were.

Given my lack of savvy, it's a minor miracle I sold anything. I've never been a confident liar (although sales is the art of telling the best part of the truth) and I never learned to dress for success. I jeopardized one of our prospective revenue sources, calling on a high-end menswear store wearing...

a leisure suit.

Hey, man, it was the SEVENTIES.

I compounded this with candor. When the client demanded, "Where's your boss today?" I answered, "Oh, he's taking one of the *big* accounts to lunch."

Everybody should be a salesperson once. The world revolves around money being persuaded to change hands, and it's instructive to see that up close.

I worked on commission and lived on a draw, a loan against whatever I brought in. This was the uncertainty of cabbing with a really big nut. If you didn't already have mood swings, that would do it.

With the pressure on, I became fairly competent at sales by zealously buying into the product. You can always give a good speech if you believe the words are true.

My usual problems selling myself were trumped by being part of something bigger. There was also some charisma hiding in the Nibble Nook drawer, and if I could keep a customer laughing, I could wear him down until he signed up just to get rid of me.

So I did okay as a salesperson, but just okay. I gave too much attention to the smaller, needier accounts. Oh, they *liked* me (always a huge ACOA trigger) they just couldn't support me.

A few shrewd retailers even managed to sell me more merchandise than they bought in spots; they were going to turn a profit either way.

But I had more up weeks than down, and only a few like that burlesque routine where one hooker asks another:

"How much did you turn in tricks?"

"A hundred dollars and fifty cents."

"Those cheapskates! Which one gave you the fifty cents?"

"They all did."

My sales days would end happily, however, with helpful fiduciary experience, a non-polyester wardrobe, and a leg up on my real dreams.

That leg was connected to the foot which was finally in the radio door, with the part that talked attached.

Years earlier I'd completed the correspondence announcing course, but the school's "placement department" turned out to be a subscription to *Broadcasting* magazine, with best wishes for a successful career.

I'd pretty much given up the notion of ever being that cool guy in the commercial.

But one April Fool's Day WXRT needed extra voices to do a skit, and I was drafted.

The *Godfather* movies were current then, and I was supposed to play the Don, showing up to take over the station. I had only two lines, but I even stuffed tissue in my cheeks.

Showtime arrived. I was so rattled I could barely get the words to come out, let alone the wheezy Sicilian accent.

I was thinking: *My God, this is a live microphone.*

But fortunately, like power outages and surgery, it was over soon.

Except for that last part (as with all things which thrilled and terrified me) where I had to prove that *I could handle it better next time.*

I had Kleenex in my mouth and a fire in my belly.

If the longest journey begins with a single step, don't knock a good proverb just because mine was channeling Marlon Brando.

Chapter Twelve

THE SOUTH

N ineteen seventy-six was the nation's Bicentennial Year. As the calendar marched toward that 200th Fourth of July, Americans got in step, making sure no one missed the significance of that anniversary, or slept through it.

Patriotic fervor reached a loud, colorful high. Brass bands got new uniforms. Civic groups painted fire hydrants red, white, and blue.

TV's *Bicentennial Minute* presented 60-second history capsules in which the Founding Fathers ruffled their powdered wigs and sent irate letters to the King of England.

Writing with feathers almost made a comeback.

And where was I during this all-American, *E Pluribus Unified* block party to celebrate common ideals? In the corner of the country that started the Civil War.

I was never in the South before. At least not in the part that wandered off from the rest of the class during the Lincoln Administration. I knew they talked funny down there, and I'd heard about the food – pulled pork barbecue, hush puppies, sweet tea, Moon Pies. Hand me that bib, Bubba.

But I wasn't there as a hungry tourist. I was living and working in the cradle the Confederacy, having been bitten by *the on-air bug.*

(This insect leaves no mark. But its venom drives the crazed bitee to zigzag the country with *Radio & Records'* classified ads and a pair of headphones. It's not an easy thing to watch.)

WXRT had demystified media for me. Once I saw how the donuts got their holes, I wanted an apron. After fantasizing for so long about being the slick voice coming out of my teenage transistor, the real thing appeared possible. I just needed an opening.

That confidence takes care of the *what*. Hedging my bet in case of catastrophe was the *where.*

The harder a thing is to do, the more rewarding its outcome. Following that logic, a big payoff is guaranteed when the prospect is impossible.

I was prepared to pay some dues. If I were going to be on the air, I'd have to start at the bottom of the bottom. And since any public proposition kept me in jitters, the more isolated the locale, the better.

Jackpot! I found a place no one ever heard of.

It wasn't easy. I read ads until I found the rare station which didn't mention on-air experience. That was a tiny outlet in a small place nestled in the rural southeastern part of the not overly large state of North Carolina. You couldn't get much farther from a population center and still be on land.

I sent the station a homemade tape, which must have sounded like some deranged kid counting down the hits from his parents' basement.

My application also got there with the tape *blank* (no idea why, unless the Postal Service was erasing suspicious packages) so the addressee may have thought I was trying to pull a fast one, or working as a mime.

After this opening move, my second tape arrived intact, and the owner must have been desperate too, because he said to come on down.

And with a Rebel Yell, I did.

The South was still the target of many dated prejudices Northerners had about that part of the country. Backwater mentality, Klan sentiments, a scarcity of teeth.

Of course, none of this proved true. Everyone I met was gracious, gentlemanly, down-to-earth, and sported admirable dental work. The family-run radio station was particularly hospitable, if a little confused as to how this Yankee from Chicago happened to wind up in their carport.

I wasn't sure either, but I had brought along appropriate Below-the-Mason-Dixon-Line business attire (I was supposed to host a show and sell spots) and a white three-piece suit seemed perfect. I looked like I was in a Tennessee Williams play as Big Daddy.

The owner and patriarch was a hard-working small-town radio man from the old school. He spent mornings calling on whatever neighbors hadn't already seen him that week, closing his gentle pitches with, "So, I thought I'd better stop by..."

Then he wound up back at the station to host the noon show, for which he played an organ – *live* – plugging all the sponsors he called "benefactors."

He was a character, and nice to me. But these good people and I weren't destined to stay together.

Things went south quickly, no pun necessary. We were just too small for each other.

My own marketing efforts were a bust. The commercial base (I remember two mobile-home dealers and a tire store) was already saturated, or had turned down radio, despite my boss's claim that newspaper ads were secondary. Why was that?

"Some folks in this area can't read too good."

I was rethinking the white suit.

Being on the air was also frustrating. In small operations (unless Mom and Pop are engineers) the equipment is generally hit-or-miss. There was often just one working turntable, so you had to cue up records while gabbing inanely with the mike open. Club deejays do this, but for a novice it was like parallel parking with your head inside a paper bag.

Those were dark weeks. Six hundred miles from Chicago seemed like the other end of the world.

But then, beginning the roller-coaster ride that would animate my stint in the southeastern United States, my luck changed.

We'd rented a house in Fayetteville, the nearest municipality, best known as the home of Fort Bragg and the 82nd Airborne. I dropped in with no appointment at the "modern country" station in town with a half-baked audition tape under my arm, and happened to show up the same day someone unexpectedly quit. They hired me on the spot.

Yee-haw!

(Speaking of which, an aircheck from that period displays some improbable version of a *Southern drawl*. Where this audio disguise came from, I can't say. Maybe I was worried the gray-and-butternut crowd would find my blue-bellied accent objectionable, so I tried to assimilate by imagining that I had a wad of Red Man under my gums.)

"Hey! That don't sound like no good ol' boy. I think he's from the North."

"You mean, like Raleigh?"

But I liked these people, and I wanted them to like me. The station turned out to be ideal for someone making a career out of a correspondence school's TV commercial. I did everything there, hosting evening and midday and afternoon music shows, creating goofy commercials, even anchoring newscasts on our FM sister station. (The PD said I "talked the news." Maybe I was on to something.)

I also got my first taste of all-talk radio by producing the station's noontime call-in program, aggressively entitled "Sound Off!"

I even got to fill in as the host one day, which included my first-ever interview. Chatting up some local dentist about a charity event, it was my life's longest hour. "Doc, we have a few minutes left. Can you tell that funny story about bicuspids again?"

The hardest part of this new job was handling the equipment, of which there were many gizmos to be fiddled with, all while timing records to hit network feeds and simultaneously trying to talk.

Not a small challenge for the kid who couldn't field a pop-up without injuries.

I had to keep one eye on this electronic maze, the other on logs that dictated what happened when, and that third one in the middle of my forehead on several clocks that counted the seconds – if I failed to execute any of the above – to when the folks packing parachutes at Ft. Bragg would hear a duet between Dolly Parton and Lumber Liquidators, or dead air.

Every shift was a battle to see how long I could go without making a technical error. On my best day that was about two hours, on my worst maybe two records. Then I would sometimes lose my temper.

Once I went off in way that should have gotten me fired. And for five tense days I waited for exactly that to happen.

I had broken the cardinal rule of broadcasting: Don't *ever* curse, swear, or use obscenity in a studio. You never know when a microphone is suddenly, maybe accidentally, going to go on the air.

(This is related to another rule: never blurt anything bad into your *own* microphone.)

In the midst of a rare, error-free show, I hit the wrong button, spoiling the afternoon's seamless technical work. I'd messed up *again*. When would I learn this board? Under my breath, I went, "Shit."

Then I saw, to my heart-pounding horror, that *my mike was still on.*

I turned it off.

And then screamed "SHITTT!" to myself for the next five minutes.

I knew I was in trouble.

Day one. I waited for the station manager to race down the hall, his face purple, my walking papers in his hand. I locked the studio door.

But nothing happened.

Whew. At least *he* hadn't heard me.

Day two. I expected a mob of angry Bible-Belters to descend on the station, loudly demanding that this foul-mouthed carpetbagger be tarred, feathered, and ridden out of town on Stephen Foster's banjo.

I locked my front door.

But nothing happened.

Did they take Sundays off?

Day three. I waited for a van from Washington carrying the entire enforcement division of the FCC to screech into the parking lot, ready to suspend the station's license and have me deported to Libya.

I locked myself in my car.

But nothing happened.

Days four and five. No recriminations, no arrests.

In fact, no one said a word. Was I actually going to get by with this heinous crime? Apparently so.

Weeks passed, and that was that. I'll never know how I managed to escape punishment for violating the Communications Act of 1934.

There are a few scenarios which might explain it.

Maybe it was just acoustics. The crescendo of a whining steel guitar kicking off the next record simply covered my on-air gaffe. I hadn't blurted an obscenity over the public airwaves *that* loud.

Or, the audience didn't hear anything off-key, thinking I'd just introduced another country record: "Now, here's Travis *Tritt*."

But in the biggest relief to my panic – and the biggest blow to my ego – maybe no objections surfaced because, at that critical and crucial moment, *no one was listening.*

Shit.

In little league they put the worst kid in right field, the least likely place someone will hit the ball. You spend the whole game hoping no one does, but when it's over you wonder if you'll ever get out of right field.

Listeners were used to surprises from that station in any case. A small market meant you could screw around some, and the maturity-challenged deejays would insert flatulent sound effects in each other's shows, or put a match to somebody's script.

Several real personalities graced the place. The entertainment kind, and ones psychologists study.

Brother S., a classic, down-home radio preacher, began our broadcast day with gospel bluegrass, but never seemed to remember what he had on the turntable. "Here's a little song by (long pause...) well, whoever it is, y'all sing *purty* now."

Brother S. kept his belongings in a mysterious little cabinet in a corner of the studio. It would have contained his well-worn records, his self-sold ad copy, and – we speculated – a burning bush.

Our boss, Paul, was the deep-throated station manager/announcer who had the best pipes south of Cape Fear. He always warmed up by intoning "*One, one, one....*" in descending notes. The windows began to rattle before he got to *two*.

We were all afraid of Jesse, the chief engineer, a former Marine drill sergeant who terrorized all us DJs by threatening to have our licenses revoked. Jesse was proud to be an anatomical phenomenon, describing himself as "a prick with ears." This was accurate.

But everyone liked the FM PD, call him Lane, a clean-cut family man and Sunday-school-teacher type, an unlikely choice to run a rock 'n' roll radio station. Lane once circulated a memo discontinuing their slogan (*"Just to turn you on"*) because he had received a tip it was some sort of drug reference.

The most talked-about performer in the building, however, wasn't a human being. It was a machine.

A tall, boxy, automation unit designed to play songs and voice tracks in lieu of a live announcer. *In lieu of a live announcer.*

This device appeared in the control room one day and then stood there looking sinister and ominous for several weeks. No one knew when it would suddenly come to life to take everyone's job away.

The tension mounted. The jocks were abuzz with speculation and anxiety. I even began a play with this robot as the protagonist. Some disturbed member of the air staff finally wigs out, dousing the automaton with gasoline. (A great stage effect, I thought, if you could just work out the blocking.)

Of course, this didn't happen in real life.

It didn't need to. The monster spun into action one morning, long enough to scramble the music and announcements. It sounded like we hired a new guy, and he'd been drinking.

There were hushed conferences and raised voices. Strangers showed up, tinkered, then left. Others came and went. Then one day this modern marvel disappeared too.

Humans had triumphed over artificial intelligence! Nobody could get it to work.

By the time all of my colleagues were breathing normally again, I was ready to graduate from this very educational institution.

But three final lessons preceded the small-school diploma.

First, in little towns, people just show up at the front door of their local radio station.

Second, no one ever looks the way you imagine from listening to them spin records.

Third, you're never too nice to get a death threat.

(And don't let anyone tell you that time moves more slowly in the South. These truths all popped up one day in the space of about five minutes.)

It was late afternoon, and the offices were already closed when someone rang the doorbell. After hours, that triggered a colored bulb in the studio, like in my old roller rink. (You'd pray COUPLES would light up, then hyperventilate when it did.)

I put on a long record and went out to see who was there. At the door stood a very large man.

"Can I, um, help you?"

"I was looking for that Garry Lee Wright."

"That's me."

"No, you're not."

This wasn't going to go well.

"Really, I'm your guy."

"*Don't put me on, son.* I listen to that ol' boy all the time, and you definitely ain't him."

I was thinking that would be fine. My visitor looked he'd missed his parole appointment, and a stage of evolution.

"What'd you want to see me – uh, *him* – about?"

"To tell that dude if he don't play my *request...*"

Aha. Now I got it. But had this disgruntled customer ever called? I couldn't place his voice. Maybe I'd missed an odd letter, something written by hand in WD-40.

"...I'm gonna git my *shotgun* off the truck."

Oh.

I looked over his shoulder to see if, by chance, a squad car might be passing at that moment. One I could signal subtly, by screaming.

There wasn't.

"You were looking for – was it Garry Lee *White,* you said? I heard he was going overseas."

"Overseas?"

"Yeah. North Korea, I think."

"You sure?"

"Leaves tomorrow. *But I'll tell him you came by.*"

Chapter Thirteen

FLORIDA

We've all observed Endless Menu Syndrome.

This diner studies the restaurant's offerings through two bread baskets, interrogates the server about sauces and side dishes, polls his tablemates about what *they're* getting, looks around the room at the plates coming to other tables, and finally, with the agony of sending a child off to preschool, makes a reluctant decision, but only after upping the ante.

"Dressing on the side, please. And do you have any braised ferns?"

Alas, when the food arrives he doesn't like it. But sullenly declines to send it back, not wanting to inconvenience anyone.

Later, he demolishes a package of stale cookies and calls it a day.

Despite the flatware and digestive system, our tablemate's behavior isn't about appetite.

It's fear.

He's afraid he'll make the wrong choice, that his decision-making equipment is defective, that he'll go wrong because *nothing* can satisfy him.

That's correct, it can't. His hunger isn't for food, but for the sweet excitement of vicariously sampling everything – *imagining* how it would be. Once he commits himself and that plate arrives, the game is over. That's why he keeps looking at the menu.

He may even be a full-blown *experience junkie*. According to experts, that's either a disease or a hobby.

Appetite and fear are powerful motivators, for good and bad. Fear of the unknown keeps our longing for newness in check – bad when it prevents us from doing something necessary or worth a calculated risk, but good when it keeps us from doing something really stupid.

Fear of the *known* is helpful too.

I had it knocked in North Carolina. But I was a glutton. I wanted to try everything. I was over my fear of the known and my fear of the unknown, and about the only thing I was still afraid of was that some interesting opportunity was out there and I was missing it.

So began a season of surprises which played out in America's Sunshine State. One surprise was, sunshine would rarely be involved.

It was a summer of firsts. Despite so many employers, I'd somehow managed to miss an ailing, failing, flailing company. Now I found one.

I would meet my first screwy bosses. ACOAs are always on the lookout for strange authority figures. I wasn't living with unpredictable people this time, just getting memos from them.

It was the first job to literally keep me up all night. And my first suspicion that wee-hours living and psychological mishaps are somehow related.

All these came my way following that spring in the Carolinas, as I was wrapping up freshman radio and dodging armed listeners.

My friend Mike had left for a Florida station, and I asked if they might have something for me. (See *"What other diners are ordering,"* above.)

And... *eureka!* This Jacksonville AMer played pop music all day but wanted, for some reason, to add an evening talk show. I didn't get details, and didn't want any. Talk had become a secret grail ever since anchoring "Sound Off!" with nothing between me and the abyss but some newspaper clips, my wits, and adrenaline. I wanted to try that hour again.

I'd also *produced* the show, which sounds pretty important. (Mostly I answered phones to screen out the worst drunks and whackos, unless we were short on callers, then the bar got somewhat lower.)

Counting the dentist, my interview experience was also extensive.

So I knew I was qualified. The program director must have thought so too, since he didn't insist on meeting me. *He actually hired me over the phone.*

When you're 25, nothing seems like a bad idea.

I'd been to Florida once before on one of those infamous family vacations, this time to Key West. It rained all week (my parents could never get a break) and I spent my time trying to build a Legos ranch house like the one pictured in the directions. It kept turning out like that barbecue Lucy Ricardo lost her wedding ring in, and had to reassemble in the dark.

By my second visit to Florida I was too old to struggle with a pesky toy. Unless you count the motorcycle I rode down there on Interstate 95.

This was no Harley Hog, by the way. My bike was a 450, easily outrun by anyone who'd been to Kenya. The highway was like riding a skateboard in a hurricane. That trip purged all my *Easy Rider* fantasies. No more envying cross-country bikers slicing through the wind in their leatherwear. By the state line I was numb from the waist down. A week later I still walked like a retired cowboy.

North Florida's marvels began as I hit town. The first was Jacksonville itself, still years away from an NFL franchise. But the ambitious city fathers had declared that the municipal boundary extended all the way to the county line. Leaving Georgia, you drove past barren, unpopulated scenery until a sign whizzed by – *Jacksonville City Limits* – which was followed by more barren, unpopulated scenery.

When a building finally appeared, mirage-like, you were downtown.

I got there at sunset. That was an omen, since it was one of the last I would see that season.

Tooling around, I noticed liquor stores doubled as bars, and even had *drive-through windows.* Pull up, get a beverage in a styrofoam cup, then speed off, a cocktail napkin and a steering wheel in each hand.

(I assume that's changed since. Or the cops just stopped giving weaving drivers sobriety tests and counted the swizzle sticks on their front seats.)

I could have used a few belts under my own the next morning, when I finally walked into my latest employer's building for the biggest surprise yet.

My new boss was now my *former* boss.

Bob had stepped down from management the same day I arrived. He said he'd decided to devote his full efforts to hosting the station's morning show, whose ratings (along with the station's, I would soon discover) were taking on water between Key West and Cuba.

What about the talk show they had hired me for? That was "on hold." (Business-speak, meaning *Great idea, Stan. Don't bring it up again.*)

I was going into shock. I was now out of *two* jobs, the one I'd quit and the one which evaporated while I was playing Hell's Angel down I-95.

All of this seemed far from possible. The phrase *healthy ambition* had sounded so redundant, I didn't know there was any other kind. It never occurred to me I might be trading a robust company for one in the ICU. Things were apparently so desperate that a "new management team" was on its way from California at that very moment.

But wait.

Like a game show host ushering some losing contestant off stage, my as-of-that-morning ex-boss had a consolation prize for me.

If I still needed a job (*if?*) I could play records in the overnight hours.

Considering the alternative, like bartending for thirsty Florida drivers, I said okay.

I should have said Legos.

Summer began. The first challenge was staying vertical from 11 at night until 5 in the morning. I would often do so in later years, but this was without warning or practice. Third-shifters know the drill: get off work when no one's around and the only thing on TV is SportsCenter. Still wired, you can't fall asleep without thinking about getting up again. Eventually you're so exhausted that you just pass out, and 20 minutes later the alarm goes off.

All-night *show* was also something of a misnomer. I would ultimately learn to work an empty room, but this was a black hole of time, six hours of short songs and not much else. I did jumping jacks to stay awake for each hour's Big Moment, which was when I read the marine weather forecast.

At a frequency apparently short on listeners, there didn't appear to be enough overnight for a hand of bridge. Only three ever surfaced when I was around, one of them a station salesman named, I swear, Walt Friend.

He had insomnia (of course, and who could blame him) when he called to say he liked my occasional bursts of personality. Not sure what those were, I appreciated the compliment anyway, although it might have been some new form of somnambulism.

There was also a woman who rang the doorbell in the middle of the night, whom I had to inform that we no longer offered 3 a.m. tours. The woman then confided that there was nothing under her raincoat. She did look a little cold.

Our third listener was some strange girl who called the request line (at least this one phoned before coming by) asking to see our "prize machine" in action. That attraction wasn't even on the daytime tour, being a sound effect. Too bad, because she wanted to show me *her* most prized possession, which was a can of rattlesnake meat.

This is why I can't write fiction.

On cue, the new executive team showed up. There should have been a puff of white smoke, but it was more like the sound of breaking glass. The general manager (whose name I can't recall even under hypnosis) brought me in and said he was going to give me a terrific career tip. He was from that first wave of consultants who parachute into a struggling company and set it right, so my ears perked up.

Now, I would get the scoop from an expert.

He popped the cork. If I wanted to get ahead...

Yes?

I should change my name.

Excuse me?

To *Garson.*

I beg your pardon?

"*Garson*. It's such a great name!" he told me, in the same excited tone you'd get from Charles Ponzi. "*I can't believe nobody's using it!*"

I don't remember if I burst out laughing or crying, or just tried to get out of his office before he advised me to become a male prostitute or adopt a ferret.

His second-in-command, my new boss, we'll call Carl. He and I were immediately suspicious of each other. For one thing, Carl looked about 13.

He also had a weird, breathless way of talking. You didn't know whether he was saying something passionately, or getting ready to cough.

Carl traveled with a library of records, which we played at a faster speed "to brighten them up." (This was a strategy developed by a successful consultant, although I always wondered how recording artists felt about that.)

Or any artist. "Aló, Jacques? Émile et ze *Louvre*. Zat Da Vinci wing, cct look so drab. Could you dab a leetle rouge on ze Mona Lisa?"

Carl's predecessor had hired me, reneged, then substituted a job I hadn't even asked for, so he and I had something in common. We were both stuck.

And destined to spend the summer together in an uncomfortable dance. He would send me my anemic, inherited, all-night ratings, and I couldn't think of anything to do but tear them up.

(You would too. Code for "too small to measure" was *-1*. My audience was not only infinitesimal, it even looked like I'd caused some deaths.)

Things couldn't get any worse, which is usually when they do. Every evening I began to develop a nagging headache that escalated until the end of the shift. Six hours nightly, the whole vexing summer.

When Elvis left the building that August, I was ready to join him.

Armchair analysts will think they've spotted a psychosomatic finale here. Solitary guy, sleep-deprived and under stress, his body playing mean tricks, his mind collapsing like an overloaded porch.

Hindsight always tells you to look ahead next time, carefully reading the menu before ordering the *cabrito.*

But I also learned not to pile on myself in times of turmoil by doubting my own sanity.

Call this: *Hey! Maybe It IS a Brain Tumor!*

Those chronic headaches weren't in my head. They weren't panic or paranoia or catastrophizing. They weren't migraines or muscle knots or sinus congestion. There was no over-the-counter remedy, or under one.

The headaches were toxic shock.

This detail emerged after I'd gone back north, throwing in the beach towel around Labor Day. (When I finally gave Carl my notice, I thought he was going to kiss me on the mouth.)

I got the story after another staffer contacted me to ask if, by chance, I'd had "unusual symptoms" while whiling away the dog days down in Florida.

Well, as a matter of fact...

Dig this. The radio station was next to a factory, and seemed to have difficulty keeping its airborne by-products under wraps during the day.

But later, when no one was looking (say, about midnight every night) the place just gave up trying *and turned off all its pollution controls.*

Unidentified particulates were thus released into the balmy air, and up my unsuspecting nose.

I wasn't the only employee with odd complaints. Some women even had irregular menstrual cycles. Would I be interested in joining a class-action suit?

Never ignore pain. It's the universe's way of getting our attention.

I would hear nothing more about the lawsuit, the station, or those smokestacks among the palms. It would be years before I tried all-night radio again, and then I would be talking to 37 states over the airwaves and around the world on something new involving computers.

I'd like to think everything else from that Florida holiday worked out for my sunny tour mates too.

That Carl eventually reached puberty, that the EPA finally sent in a SWAT team, and that the general manager made a killing as a life coach.

But the subconscious retains the Tilt-A-Whirl rides of our youth, and I do have a recurrent dream.

The doorbell rings. Standing there is a woman, naked except for a Federal Express cap.

She hands me a wet package covered with soot.

Inside is a gin-and-tonic in a styrofoam cup, a can of rattlesnake meat, and a picture of Walt Friend wearing a Speedo.

Then she has me sign for everything, and I write "Garson."

Chapter Fourteen

MORNING IN AMERICA

Count your blessings – twice, to check the math.

We all talk about luck, but no one really wants to believe in it. We like to say we make our *own* luck, that we control our own lives. It's unsettling to think some unseen hand might actually be pulling the levers.

Or, God forbid, that everything is random.

Ironically, the most spectacular recipients of fortune are its biggest deniers. Some people are simply born with a pair of loaded dice. They get what they want early on, then spend their lives thinking the rest of us don't work hard enough.

At the other end are folks who buy piles of lottery tickets but never manage to pick a winner. The people who seem to depend on luck the most don't have any.

The rest of us occupy more of a middle ground. We believe in luck *sometimes* and have stretches of good and bad that balance out. In fact, luck stays in the background most of the time. Like the lighting in a room, we don't notice it until it changes.

But an unexpected event gets our attention.

Wow! A parking space.

Or: Did someone actually *tow my car?* I thought it was right here next to the giant Indian statue.

Fluky moments come and go, but windfalls and pitfalls always test our slippery belief in fate. Bad decisions mean *asking* for bad luck, of course, which is actually comforting. We can always blame destiny when we screw something up.

But even good decisions need happenstance. Dozens of guys were ready to invent the light bulb, but Edison was the one who could get financing.

Too much good fortune can be really dangerous. We forget the coin has two sides. Tails after heads is as inevitable as the back of a horse appearing after the front of one.

So when does confidence become foolishness? How far can you push your luck until it trips over the ottoman? In my 20s the dice changed so rapidly I couldn't tell if I was rolling them myself or just trying to get a bet down in time.

That white-knuckle patch wound through the 1970s for the world in general. It was a gooey, fondue pot of a decade, when people knew the words to "Me and You and a Dog Named Boo" and refrigerators came in harvest gold and avocado.

I was in a wedding then. The ceremony included folk music and a reading from *The Prophet*. The gift china was dark green. I wore a brown tuxedo.

That's right, *brown*. It's an earth color.

Not to bury the lead, but I should probably mention that the groom in that wedding was me.

The bride and I met on a blind date while we both worked in the Wrigley Building. She was smart, funny, and the first normal person I ever went out with. We shared a taste for classical music and Monty Python and Scrabble. We meshed the way only people in their 20s can mesh. We knew each other three weeks before we decided to get married.

Our first shared residence was in a big Chicago apartment building near the lake, where I rented an orbital sander and refinished the living room floor.

(I was always trying to make some compass point *home*. Landlords, if your tenants are nomads, they'll wreck the place or double your investment.)

We moved south, and were both stranded in Florida when that expansive summer contracted. Then, as I mentioned, fate filled my sails.

I can't rag on the difficult bosses I've had without appreciating the ones who kept me afloat when I wandered off from the rest of the snorkelers. I made a call to the Midwest, and my old WXRT superiors told me to come back if I wanted. I could sell time as before, and there might even be some on-air opportunities. I went from utter desperation to a really good mood in fifteen minutes.

Back to Chicago we moved, this time into a wood-shingled complex on West Drummond that looked like a Swiss chalet. My obsessive decorating might have led to an attractive ski lift, but I had to get back to work. I settled for some light painting and stashed my waterbed in a spare room.

WXRT was also hanging on to hippiedom. The air staff still chose most of the music; the loose format protected listeners from an overdose of creativity. Say, no more than three drum solos an hour.

But they managed to stay to the left of everybody else, and the connoisseur could still look forward to an entire set of songs with *rodeo* in the title.

I nearly missed my chance to ride along. Ramping up to a weekend show, I was supposed to submit sample lists, but anxiety tripped me up. I knew as much as anyone who listens to records all week, but I kept thinking: *Someone will find fault with this. They'll see I don't know what I'm doing.*

I began putting off my air debut, claiming I needed to concentrate on sales.

"You can't start this week either?"

"Sorry, another big meeting with The Rug Joynt."

This went on until it was obvious I was having second thoughts about going into a studio again. They told me it was now or never.

I debuted on a Saturday morning, my voice cracking so badly it sounded like the transmitter was on fire.

My mother, listening in Indiana, had never heard me on the radio before. She said she cried. I don't know if this was from pride or embarrassment.

Thus began one of the most spine-tingling times of my life, when rewards seemed to come on spec and old obstacles popped up in new guises.

To begin with, I bombed but succeeded anyway. We like to say no one will believe in you more than you believe in yourself, but those first few months were an exception to that otherwise durable rule. I was over my head, acting a role I hadn't rehearsed. Fortunately the character's motivation was simple.

Don't blow it now, because everybody's looking.

But I was convinced I was flopping. It wouldn't have been much of a surprise to get taken aside.

"We gave it a try, Garry, but..."

Then the strangest thing happened.

They promoted me.

I was genuinely stunned. The rock format had gone 24 hours, and the first morning host was being lured by a competitor. They offered me the show.

This development was either too good to be true or too true to be good. I couldn't think up an excuse fast enough. They liked my "wit and commentary." I didn't know I was providing these. I just thought I was trying to keep my hands from shaking.

But the press release went out, and I was in.

My tour on the dawn patrol began.

Morning radio is the high-intensity light that illuminates the bedrooms, bathrooms, kitchens, and front seats of humanity at their least conscious. It can precede a first cup of coffee. It appears out of nowhere when the clock reaches some prearranged hour, a genie that springs to life fully awake and alert, ready to blaze the trail of a new day on behalf of a grateful, and sometimes adoring, population.

Behind the scenes, the host of that miracle is the lowest-ranking servant in a Victorian household. The Irish kid who shivers his way out of bed before everybody else, then has to trudge downstairs to where the coal is and start a fire from scratch.

It was a jolt, getting up at 3 a.m. every day to make my way to an all-night diner, where I flogged myself into eating two poached eggs and perusing the newspapers for wit-triggering, commentable news stories while drinking three cups of tea and trying to find the funny button.

I wound up at the station at 5 a.m. to pull four hours of music, agonizing over every choice.

Which wasn't necessary. Mostly I just had to keep the vinyl coming, occasionally trading quips with Charles (C.D.) Jaco, then Charlie Meyerson.

Both were destined for big things, as was our sportscaster Bruce Wolf. Norm Winer too, who came on as program director then and didn't fire me.

Terri Hemmert held forth in middays, still does.

Bobby Skafish did nights, the hippest punk in town.

Those Carter-Reagan years were fertile. Jimmy got elected promising never to lie. This became a problem when he said we were having a *malaise*, which sounded awful because no one knew what it meant. The Gipper replaced him by promising never to use unfamiliar words, or to act sad on TV.

Those were satisfying days. At night I went to a lot of concerts, got to emcee a few, and met some of the listeners I had only imagined talking to. Seeing 20,000 people from the stage for the first time was heart-stopping, and loud.

Most of my day was spent á la nerd, however, producing pieces of parody and sketch comedy which became my act. Every morning I would try to come up with something for the following day, sometimes dragging people in from the hallway to do voices. I thought I was Orson Welles.

It was late-70s-style satire, or supposed to be. A spoof called "Canal Acres" featured an alien voice hawking tracts of land in the burgeoning real-estate boom on Mars. The hook: "A year-round tan!"

A foreign-language course included a narrator who became impatient with the slow-witted learner, then insulted him in conversational French.

"The Love El" echoed TV's *The Love Boat*. Complete with a catchy theme song, it imagined commuters finding kinky sex on the transit system.

One effort – *unintentionally* controversial – was a spot for the upcoming visit of Pope John Paul II. *Forget Elvis. Forget Jagger. It's the Pope... LIVE!* (We got one irate phone call, but just remember that His Holiness had a record out at the time.)

For April Fool's, I did an hour in Spanish, playing "Oye Como Va" and "La Bamba." Fourth of July, I narrated a spectacular fireworks display over our parking lot at 7 o'clock in the morning. The entire Declaration of Independence, with only one typo.

When you're in the right place, humor is everywhere. Doing street interviews, I didn't even have to make up the punch lines.

"Have you ever heard of Frank Zappa?"

"No, but we're from Michigan."

The moment it dawned on me I was finally in show business – a professional *creator* – I was hunched over some pre-digital tape deck, grease pencil in hand, marking the last splice of something I thought was clever, and I realized I was living everyone's secret dream. To get paid money for just screwing around all day.

I had made it to the top.

Of something.

Wee-hours oblivion in north Florida to morning drive on the most with-it station in Chicago took just two years. You'd have to call it a meteoric rise.

Stay tuned for gravity.

All my life, confidence has either trailed the job I had or made me want more. I couldn't get the needle to stay put in the middle. Being picked out of the crowd to entertain such a special part of it, I'd fallen asleep in a pile of leaves and woke up as Commissioner of Baseball.

It was a huge leap for someone in his twenties (and only chronologically) and my mood swings made me an undependable funnyman. Some days I couldn't imagine how I'd ever gotten into this.

They'll be on to me soon. I can't fake it much longer.

I needed constant reassurance. That's another ACOA trait, the promiscuous approval-seeker. Someone who's so insecure he lets others (friends, enemies, people at Walgreens) decide his real value.

"We just met, but I already see you're an idiot."

"You're *right!* But how did you figure it out so quickly?"

Despite many achievements and victories, such a person still waits, *expects*, to be unmasked. To have his real and imagined shortcomings validated. It's not just insecurity. There's actually a name for this: *Impostor Syndrome*.

That phenomenon, identified by Pauline Clance and Suzanne Imes in *The Impostor Phenomenon Among High Achieving Women,* found successful professionals who secretly thought they'd just been lucky, or conned someone. They constantly looked over their shoulders, expecting to be exposed.

That book came out the same year (1978) I would begin proving that its principles also applied to men.

Failures seemed well-deserved, but successes were surprising, temporary spikes in the system that wouldn't last. I couldn't accept that – at least part of the time – I *caused* good things to happen.

Judith Albright, an EFT practitioner, writes:

"It is estimated that 30% of the population has some form of (Imposter Syndrome), particularly highly successful people....

"Messages conveyed from an early age by our parents, teachers and other significant people in our lives...families who impose unrealistic standards; families who are very critical; families who are ridden with conflict and anger; families whose expectations are in conflict with their children's career aspirations.

"The imposter syndrome is like a set of handcuffs that prevents smart and talented people from (moving) beyond 'safe' dead end jobs because they are afraid to take risks. Others never make as much money as they want or get the promotions they could have had because they secretly believe they are frauds who don't 'deserve' to have financial success or be rewarded."

Chimes sounded when I read this. I didn't know I was a pioneering impostor.

Insidiously, a different part of my miswired brain told me at the same time I was *too* good, that what I needed was to get out from behind the records and become a talk personality.

The praise I craved wouldn't come as long as I was mostly off-mike, waiting to back-announce a set by the real stars.

(There's art and skill to being a good disc jockey. Musicology, plus the discipline to paint on a finite canvas. I never acquired these abilities. When I was on the radio, I just wanted to run my mouth.)

Talk was where the action and attention was, and no one exemplified that more than Steve Dahl, opposite whom I worked during his 1979 Disco Demolition. That stunt made him a national name, and I would read his exploits every morning as I prepared to go on the air myself, eating my poached eggs at what sometimes seemed like the kiddie table.

(I didn't understand the concept of *competition* then, except the part where other guys run by you.)

But one event that year was what they call life-changing. On St. Patrick's Day, 1979 my son was born. I'd never pictured myself as a father, and couldn't quite believe it. I kept a Polaroid of him clipped to my visor.

So these were the ricocheting balls already in play when another one suddenly came down the chute.

Five years had passed since I'd been on stage as a performer in my own right, that busted audition at The Spot. Suspecting that my off-key singing and sounds-like-he's-wearing-gloves musicianship were holding me back (even denial has its limits), I'd put my live career on hold until I could work up the nerve to get out from behind my guitar and actually *face* the audience, just me and them.

Secretly, that is. But a local comic, Ed Fiala, encouraged me to try standup. *Other people do it, why not you?*

Ed's cronies took me to the aptly named Comedy Womb in Lyons, insisting I get up and do some material. I was a wreck. My legs were shaking so badly they told me to sit down on stage, then introduced me as a *humorist*, trying to alert the room that something different was coming.

"What is he, paralyzed?"

"They said he's a 'humorist.'"

"Do we laugh or not?"

I did a routine about the movie *Urban Cowboy,* where John Travolta tames a mechanical bronco. My idea was called *Suburban Cowboy.*

He had to stay on a riding lawnmower.

I taped my little set, listened the next morning, and was shocked.

I had gotten laughs. Without the guitar.

It was the sweetest song ever recorded. I played the tape a dozen times that day. After a while it sounded like Lenny Bruce at Carnegie Hall.

One fateful evening. Had I bombed that first night (and many future ones would be short on hilarity) I might have given up comedy permanently.

But my unexpected victory just added another distraction and infatuation to everything that was already spinning around me. Something had to give, and it turned out to be the morning radio show.

I stepped down with no warning, blindsiding my bosses, my colleagues, and my listeners.

(One, in that era of Communist upheaval, wrote in to ask why I had been "purged.")

I set him straight; no counterrevolutionaries had marched into XRT. But since I had nothing else immediately lined up, it was still like Shelley Long leaving *Cheers* to star in *Troop Beverly Hills.*

You could say I had a nervous breakdown, and some people did. You could say it was my first Saturn Cycle, which sounds even nuttier than the nervous breakdown theory.

You could say I broke a rule: *Don't give up what you already have just because you want more.*

Or you could say I was only following my heart. We all respect that, even when it's irrational.

In any case, I was off again.

Heh heh.

I packed for the only place in America bigger than L.A. or Chicago. And in an ironic dénouement, I ran out the clock coaching aspiring DJs at a vocational school. The first thing I told those kids about careers in broadcasting was how to avoid one.

BACK TO SCHOOL, 3001
Teachers want a raise, before it's too late

"Children! Settle down now, turn off those voice-simulation devices, and reconnect to your seating modules. And Tommy 2X, you stop eating that semiconductor paste!"

"Ewww, Ms. Frances! It's coming out his *nose.*"

"Tommy! I'm going to–"

"Ms. Frances, Billy Y2K keeps pulling my hair and saying I have a chromium deficiency!"

"Billy, do you want to go to the principal's office again and have your DNA reconfigured?"

"Ms. Frances, she called me a *mutant lifeform*!"

"Jennifer, would you like it if Billy made fun of your third eye?"

"No..."

"All right, then. All of you *behave.* And Victor 4XLT, take off that prosthetic head right now. You can morph in front of the girls at recess."

"Ms. Frances! I think I need to go to the waste elimination quadrant."

"*Again?* Well, hurry up. And remember to use the hygiene synthesizer."

"Can Mary Alice 7Q come with me?"

"*No.* Now we're wasting valuable time. I hope all of you brought the supplies that were on the list."

"My parental units said they can't afford a new spectrometer every year."

"Then you'll have to use someone else's. I'm still buying my own pencils."

"What's a 'pencil'?"

"*Never mind.* Now, listen up. The Intergalactic Education Tribunal has mandated a new curriculum so you can all get jobs out in the real solar system. We're studying Advanced Microwave Defrosting and Windows 3000 Repair."

"That's *baby* stuff! We're in fourth grade now."

"I know, they're on a back-to-basics kick. And no more social promotions, so you'd all better learn to plagiarize. We're also back to New Math."

"What's that?"

"Adding numbers without a piezoelectric abacus. For example, two plus two. Does anyone know what two plus two equals?"

"22?"

"Four thousand?"

"The Ottoman Empire?"

"No! *Can't any of you add two plus two?*"

"I know! I know! Two plus two equals four."

"That's correct, Sara. And how come *you* know so much?"

"I was home schooled when we lived on Pluto."

"That sounds nice. I wish I were there now."

"Do you want me to help the other kids?"

"Yes. Shout out your answers during those standardized tests."

Chapter Fifteen

NEW YORK

In theory, people read nonfiction to be informed, and fiction to escape.

Not always. I learn plenty from the addled imaginations of others, and my favorite break from reality is to time-travel inside a history book. No getaway is more complete than someone else's pleasures, problems, and pantaloons.

We know how the past looked, who said what, and even how food probably tasted. But *olfactory* history isn't recordable. We can only imagine how the world smelled.

Consider: fossil fuels afire, cigar smokers everywhere, horses doing their business in the street. Bearded men in derby hats wearing wool suits to baseball games in the middle of summer.

Everyone looks tense in those Matthew Brady photographs. They were waiting out the camera's long exposure, and trying not to gag.

New York City had lost some of its melting pot aromas by the time I arrived, a hundred years after the 1880s, but had acquired a few modern ones.

The Subway chain was then going international, but New Yorkers wouldn't associate that word with anything you'd want to put on a sandwich.

The atmosphere of too many people in too small a place, however, was masked – for me, and for earlier immigrants – by a more intoxicating scent.

Unlimited possibility. That's what New York smelled like.

Turning 30, I was still young enough to think any fantasy I could cook up might actually come true. And here I was in this place where everyone felt the same way. Jazz musicians had called their venues *apples,* and this was the big one.

People from Chicago are supposed to hate New York and New Yorkers, and many do. The bad blood started with the Second City rivalry, plus the perception that Midwesterners were hard-working, right-thinking caretakers of America's dreams, while Easterners were schemers, snobs, and assholes.

This isn't completely true.

Baseball, as always, played a role. Fans across the country hated the corporate Yankees, who just made things worse by winning every year.

And after 1969, Chicagoans *really* hated the Mets.

So here's my guilty secret. I loved New York. Did and always will. I love it the way you can only love a place which doesn't actually exist.

Before I ever saw Manhattan, Brooklyn, Queens, or the Bronx, I visited them many times in that city you'd call Book New York. Where Holden Caulfield and seven Glass children grew up in apartments.

Apartments. I didn't see too many of those as a small-town kid. It was usually houses or trailers. Sometimes tents.

It got me that a big, noisy family could call an apartment *home*, with books on the nightstands, soda spots on the ceiling, and pet stains on the rugs. That its inhabitants could be so *cosmopolitan.* They told each other Zen parables, and went to museums on the subway, and took taxis to play tennis.

I'd also grown up in Movie New York, where *Miracle on 34th Street* was set (my all-time favorite film, if you really want to know) where little Natalie Wood watched that Thanksgiving parade from *her* apartment, and I heard about Macy's and Bellevue and a little house out on "the Island."

Movie New York thrilled me, even when it became seedy and menacing, like Dustin Hoffman dying of whatever that was in *Midnight Cowboy.*

Rich visitors were more rousing. Myrna Loy and William Powell reading *The Thin Man*'s telegrams in their chichi hotel suite, boozing their way through Christmas Eve.

Most of all I loved TV New York, where even squalor looked interesting. I could imagine living in Ralph and Alice Kramden's Bensonhurst walk-up, with the dresser and the fire escape and the icebox. Viewers sent drapes to CBS so Alice could decorate that dump. They imagined living there too.

And what a treat, home sick from school, when I heard the bongos introducing *I Love Lucy,* set in a tidy Manhattan apartment building whose address, I would learn, was in the middle of the East River.

They didn't seem to mind, and neither did I.

It was a little disconcerting when the Ricardos and the Mertzes moved to Connecticut, but that was apparently New York too. The Petries lived up in New Rochelle, with Rob commuting in to write that TV show with Buddy and Sally. All they needed was a typewriter, some coffee, and a *prune danish*, two words I'd never heard in the same sentence.

Their cozy office was the first I'd ever seen, and it looked like the ideal job. Who wouldn't want to be a comedy writer?

Early TV dealt in fantasy, of course, and modern urban living was later portrayed through the more realistic lenses of *Taxi* and *Seinfeld* and *Friends,* and other contemporary New York shows that were shot in California.

But all those media images were trumped by the New York that still stood, exuding soot and glitter, when I finally saw it in real life.

Radio City had talked to the whole country. Rockefeller Center still did. Grand Central Station was recognizable from a thousand angles. Broadway too. Times Square was history itself. The Stork Club was gone, but Greenwich Village looked (I imagined) not much different from when Bob Dylan had lived there, a kid folksinger. Leonard Bernstein and Andy Warhol were still alive.

But New York in the 1980s was trying to rebuild itself and its reputation. America's Mecca, its Metropolis, was sprawling, teeming, *appalling.*

The capital of the globe was dirty and unsafe. (It had always been dirty and unsafe, but for some reason that seemed like a news bulletin.) Tabloids narrated the outrage and mayhem.

No one wanted to live there, and everyone did.

We got to town just as the leaves were turning. We would stay 13 years.

Me and the girl I went there with, whose name was Laurie.

She and I had met at one of the ticket-and-dinner giveaways which the station concocted. Those were always themed. If we sponsored something having to do with pirates, we lined up a restaurant serving seafood. And encouraged the winner to show up with a peg leg.

Once we awarded passes to a play about Czechoslovakia struggling under communism. Prize part two would have been a Czechoslovakian dinner, had such a thing been available.

"I don't see anything. It goes from 'Cantonese' to 'Dining with Kids.'"

"There's *nothing* from Eastern Europe?"

"How about Polish?"

"Get a table for twelve."

The play was fine, the *pierogies* were good, and everyone enjoyed their pleasant evening behind the Iron Curtain. One listener brought along his wife, who had long brown hair, blue eyes, and was sixteen inches shorter than me. Her whole face lit up when she laughed, good news for someone who imagined himself wearing floppy shoes. I'd never met anyone like her.

Laurie was a Catholic-school alumna from the South Side, the sort of institution that measured skirt lengths and hoped their graduates would be nuns. The eldest of five siblings, her grandparents had stepped off a boat at Ellis Island.

She always seemed to be in a good mood, making her about the only happy person I'd ever gotten close to – if you define happiness as being in positive spirits most of the time, which seems as good a description as any.

The couples double-dated, and when Laurie and I crossed paths again after those relationships ended, we began hanging out. Maybe it was the power of rock 'n' roll, but one night, listening to *Born to Run*, it seemed like we were in love.

We took a trip to New York City together, and stayed at the Grammercy Hotel, a kitschy place where the Rolling Stones had once partied. They'd checked out by then, but we had a pretty good time by ourselves.

Kid tourists on the loose, we walked across the Brooklyn Bridge and went to the top of the Empire State Building and took the Staten Island Ferry and had drinks in a place called *Windows on the World.*

From up there you saw a little green chip in the harbor that turned out to be the Statue of Liberty.

We had such a great time, when we got back they took away my American Express card.

(I never got another one, not in all these years. I was too chagrined to ask, and losing the original seemed like an event worth remembering.)

We liked New York so much – liked *being there together* so much – we decided to move, just like that. Twenty-somethings travel light. Lucky that first shared vacation wasn't to Mogadishu.

Our temporary home was a hotel room across from Penn Station, under Madison Square Garden. (Penn Station, not the hotel, although that wouldn't have made it any louder.) The street below was a 24-hour-a-day riot. Traffic jammed, horns honked, sirens never stopped. We didn't know the city yet, assuming it was a typical residential neighborhood.

Venturing outside, one didn't stroll. Keep up with the river of pedestrians or be run over. The locals didn't pause even to eat. They gobbled in motion. Hot dog stands, pretzel vendors, roasted-chestnut guys. Half the city dined in fancy restaurants, and the other half was afraid to sit down.

New Yorkers got off on being survivors. They were martyrs, gladiators, the last stubborn breed of urban squatters. They took pride in inhabiting an uninhabitable place. They all bounced between helping each other out and rubbing it in.

Now I was one of these hurried, harried citizens. I wasted no time starting my bright new career in this city of spotlights. Within a week I was on stage as a New York City standup comedian.

Maybe hold the applause for just a moment.

This wasn't an engagement with my name on the marquee in any size type. I had stopped in at a *showcase club*, which meant some nondescript back room with a few tables and a microphone. New performers could be found there working out their acts, in front of other new performers who were there working out their acts. If a civilian was anywhere in the room, he was somebody's uncle.

(I eventually developed a line: "Welcome to our showcase club! If you enjoy newcomers testing their skills, have your appendix out at a showcase *hospital*.")

But that came later. My first night in the big time was the worst few moments I've ever not enjoyed on stage. The only good thing was it ended quickly.

I already knew that here, where the *Tonight Show* began, were some slightly tougher rooms than Senese's Winery in Oak Lawn. In fact I was so apprehensive about this end of the pool, past the pollywog floats, that all I could do to prepare was work up my nerve. I ran out of time before I could, like, you know, write something down.

Every performance, even a phone call, needs a mission, a plan, and a rehearsal. Run through it, if only in your head. This little piggie went 0 for 3.

I was on stage less than a minute. My opening got no audible response. I couldn't *see* the audience either, because this place had real stage lighting, right in your eyes, and I wasn't used to that professional feature. I sprouted my first case of what even actuaries know is called *flop sweat*.

I couldn't think of anything to do but get off. And I did, in the middle of a sentence.

(A sidebar was following young Gilbert Gottfried, who was about to join *SNL*. He was uproarious, and would quack the Aflac duck until mistweeting.)

That first evening in a Manhattan nightclub, such a spectacular disaster, proved that the worst failures teach the best lessons. And doing *everything* wrong in one concentrated effort turned out to be a shortcut to seeing how to do it right.

That also came later, about two decades.

But first I had to lie in bed for a week, depressed, dismayed, and thoroughly defeated.

Comedy, it's all drama.

Not to ruin the suspense, but eventually I got up. Hitting a wall, for bipolars and others, demands that some part of you remember that you've been there before. If you can just see your way to getting dressed, the tumblers are in play. The longest journey begins with a single pair of pants.

I tabled standup for the time being, knocking on other doors. Radio in market one was a ways off (seven years, requiring a sequence of improbable events) but thinking I might get voiceover work in commercials, I took a tape around to agents' offices.

My first peek inside those mythical waiting rooms was just what we imagine: stage mothers with little girls in ballet tutus, big ones with head shots as Blanche DuBois.

The best meeting was with a busy woman who got confused that I was a voice actor, not some guy looking for work as a male model. She kept telling me that my beard would *have to go.* They weren't showing facial hair that year.

Like every small-town kid chasing stardom, I soon discovered I wouldn't be discovered soon enough. I'd need a real livelihood. (*Five* such positions, all odd, were impending. Please stand by.)

But I had reached some sort of plateau. I was finally a no-illusions, matter-of-fact, down-to-earth resident of Gotham.

Just like Batman.

Those first years in the city that never sleeps ended with a beginning.

On July 30, 1982, Laurie and I were married in a civil ceremony at New York City Hall. You've seen those marble pillars. It's where the hero lawyer saves Santa Claus in *Miracle on 34th Street*.

Our wedding day also had its cinematic moments.

Laurie was four months pregnant that midsummer afternoon. Our first daughter would be born three days after Christmas. (This confluence of events helped me keep several holidays straight for years.)

But that was just timing. Getting married was as inevitable as a rainbow following a thunderstorm. We were hooked on each other.

It was a hot day. We took the subway into lower Manhattan. Being new to the city, we had no friends yet, hence no attendants to invite.

In fact we had to borrow a witness from the couple who came in behind us. Her name was Mercedes Suarez – we'll always remember it – and she was nice enough to do double duty at no extra charge. She probably figured it was that kind of day.

The waiting room was filled with what could only be described as an assembly line of lovebirds in a hurry. Groomsmen and maids of honor fanned each other with newspapers. Hands were held, tenderly, across plastic chairs.

This wasn't exactly what you'd call a *chapel*. It had the warm glow of that special place you'd go for an international driver's license.

But at least the line kept moving.

Our moment came. They called our names and ushered us into an inner room, where we were greeted, sort of, by the aged, dour, overworked, weary-looking justice of the peace. We dubbed him Lance Romance.

There was no organist.

It would be libelous to say Lance was impaired while executing his official duties, but he did appear slightly glassy-eyed, juggling our names the first time through. Fortunately we knew them from memory, and gently corrected him, although New York may still have us down as Laura and Barry.

We tried to repeat something he mumbled – which *sounded* like vows, although we may have been agreeing to have our incomes garnished – and he then mispronounced us husband and wife.

A wonderful wedding, meaning full of wonder. Laurie was radiant ("The Bride Wore Black") and I had on my good shoes. We may have missed the Hokey Pokey, but there were no videotaped cake tragedies, and the only out-of-control guest was Lance.

The best moment of our momentous afternoon came in that waiting area for goo-goo-eyed couples, when out of nowhere there appeared

a maintenance guy wearing a DayGlo jumpsuit and goggles – who proceeded to mop the entire floor with disinfectant.

The city must have been worried that someone might catch something in that high-traffic tunnel of love, and it wouldn't be the bride's bouquet.

Don't be misled. This was the most romantic, most metaphysical touch we could have asked for. DayGlo Man (an apparition, really) symbolized the appearance of Jesus at that wedding in Cana. Instead of water to wine it was water to Pine-Sol. And as his consecrated bucket clinked along, you could hear the angels getting their wings.

We spent our honeymoon night packing to move to Staten Island. We would live there ten years, bookended by the births of our daughter and her sister, more easy math. They're both taller than their mother, by about six or seven inches.

Thanks again, Mercedes. We hope your friends turned out as lucky as we did. Life partners, and a pretty good story to tell.

"How did you ever wind up with someone like Garry?"

"I won him in a contest."

Chapter Sixteen

FIGHTING FOR LAUGHTER

Attack means the same thing in different contexts, but just barely. Pearl Harbor was a surprise *attack*. The Senate will *attack* inflation after their vacation. Horace *attacked* the fettucine alfredo while his wife chatted up the violinist.

I've sampled various attacks, some unexpected. I was standing in line once at a drug store when I saw (or didn't see) a young man come up to me and, without warning, slug me in the head.

My peripheral vision picked up only a blur before I felt a thud and hit the floor. The next thing I remember the woman behind the counter was asking, "Are you all right?" with a lot less surprise in her voice than seemed appropriate.

"What happened?" I asked, dizzy but curious.

"Oh, that was just Billy," she explained. "He lives in the neighborhood."

Those goofy kids! But what can you do?

About 20 years before that I was at a party when some drunken reveler came out of the crowd and announced, "I'm going to punch you in the face."

What? I wasn't sure I'd heard him right. Then, *wham*. His fist connected with my chin.

This was more weird than painful, but I left soon after, and never did find out what his problem was. (Maybe he couldn't get anyone to dance. Not all girls are attracted to a guy with a box of Marlboros rolled up under his sleeve.)

And before that I was at a truck stop with Marty when another guy (right, never seen him before either) walked up to the table and shoved his fist right in my face: "How'd you like to get smacked?"

This time, given notice, I was prepared.

And definite. "I wouldn't like that."

He smirked, as in, "I *thought* not."

Then marched away, victorious.

It obviously made his night. So I managed to avoid another out-of-the-blue attack, and even got to finish my coffee. Sometimes things go your way.

A person might ask: Why do I attract random assailants? My size (historically 6' 5" but I seem to be shrinking) probably makes me a visible target.

Or it's defective karma. Maybe I subconsciously transmit something that cries out for retaliation, and I *invite* assaults. All I know is, if a disturbed youngster or a drunken sociopath is slinking around, they'll pass up a lot of people who deserve to get whopped in the head until they come to me.

Being a nonviolent sort, I tried to protect myself with a mouth instead of fists. But words sometimes got scrambled, and my tongue didn't always work.

I used to have a slight stammer when excited, and I once began a high school speech saying, "Some of we students have trouble with English."

Even after I became a budding cut-up, I was always afraid of recrimination. Would I get in trouble? Are you *sure*?

It was inevitable that standup comedy, with its pathological blend of approval and disaster, would call out to me. It was fear of heights plus the exhilaration of leaping off a diving board. I had to prove I could survive on stage or spend the rest of my life admitting I was chicken.

Some would say I was brave. Others, needy.

But if you buy the idea that each of us is in the business of show, trying to get this or that across, the following won't seem completely unfamiliar.

Performing balances aggression and defense. You fence with all the people who are watching and listening, then fence with their consensus of how you're doing. In any give-and-take, peril lurks. Everyone knows stage slang is warfare.

I bombed. I killed. They were all on the floor, screaming. When things didn't click, *I died.*

HELP! MEDIC!

I mean, hey, you folks wanna hear another one?

Learning to aggress and defend at the same time was a life skill I didn't begin to master until the bullring of New York. Laurie and I both picked up a lot there, not always on purpose. She quickly lost her Midwestern accent, and began to sound like Marisa Tomei in *My Cousin Vinny*.

I developed a taste for bialys and egg creams, and started wearing dark shirts and light ties to exude confidence. It worked. I looked like a hoodlum.

We moved to Brooklyn, probably inevitable. Our new landlord was an arm-twisting type-A operator, aptly named Mrs. Hammer. After signing a lease and forking over a deposit, we were floored when she reneged on an agreement to finish renovating. I suggested we put our rent in escrow. She blinked.

In New York you had to fight for everything. I was figuring out that this was why the locals acted like they had hemorrhoids.

We commuted on the standing-room-only subway to Manhattan. My son attended a preschool across from the United Nations. Every morning I would carry him on the transit system. He learned his first numbers and letters waiting on the platform, reading them off the cars as they pulled in. Nothing makes the ABCs come alive like graffiti and sparks.

My son was also fascinated by our next door neighbors and their large, talkative parrot. They had prominent, *r*-challenged East Coast accents, and I thought the parrot did too.

Our neighborhood was still Old New York. You bought bread from a baker, meat from a butcher, and produce at a *greengrocer*. Missing only were an organ grinder and a monkey.

We moved into a "garden" apartment (I kept forgetting that term meant "below ground" instead of "lush") and I knocked out speculative projects on a teacher's desk that occupied most of the bedroom.

A play, *Big Plans*, was a satire about a game show host who runs for president. Ahead of its time or behind it, the farthest that it got was someone representing Dick Shawn, who played Hitler in the original *Producers* movie. Dick passed away soon after that, and I don't know if he ever read my play. Or if he did, and that was the final straw.

Radio Shmadio was another ambitious try, a sketch-comedy series I wrote scripts and even hired a cast for, which never made it to the airwaves. We came up with some good bits though. My partner Michael Sklaroff was a talented guy who'd been an extra on *Saturday Night Live*. But I couldn't sell enough stations to make it fly. Actually, any.

There was one taker, but he got demoted.

I even put some material together for *SNL* itself, sent to its founding head writer, the notorious Michael O'Donoghue. My unsolicited submission came back intact and apparently unread. They didn't ask if I had any other stuff.

There was a glimmer of success, though, even if I didn't see it at the time. The best element in that package was probably a parody of postage-paid reply cards, which also came back – and with O'Donoghue's own handwriting across the bottom: *"I have all the writers I need."*

That media artifact would be worth something today, had I kept it. But I didn't know I was a *player* then; I just thought I was being rejected. (Résumés should have two columns. Jobs we got, and ones we can brag that *we just barely missed.*)

If no one wanted my jokes, the alternative was doing them myself. I browbeat the inner children hiding in my closet into getting back on stage, and started haunting entry-level comedy venues.

The Eagle Tavern was a typical arena, just a noisy bar with a back room. And *arena* was the right word. We were all there to engage in combat.

You had to fight the producer for stage time, fight with each other for the group's favor, then fight a vibrant assortment of personal shortcomings when your turn for attention came. Just like in any office.

Although this one had most of the lights off. And in the dark we mentally rehearsed and revised our acts as we admired or cringed at everybody else's.

Okay, this guy's funny, that last one was just dirty, and this next one – I've seen him – is actually nuts.

Watching the regulars push their own envelopes week after week meant a predictable uncertainty. One night a loosely wrapped guy named Stig did a hair-raising improvisation *while walking across the entire room over people's tabletops.*

I have to say, he didn't kick over anyone's glass until the very end.

I became a master of these ceremonies. With my height, radio-ey voice, and fake fearlessness (I was getting used to stage fright by then, and made my bombing cute, á la Johnny Carson) I fancied myself a host.

And they let me emcee. Warming up a room from scratch, saving it between spotty acts, getting the hecklers to shut up or just pass out. Show business!

This led to more places with better food. My favorite was China Chalet, a block from Wall Street (right, a Chinese restaurant, the fine entertainment happened between bites from a pu pu platter). It was a pretty upscale place, though, featuring lovely Mandarin art and ideograms which I translated as, "You must ask for water."

I tried to be classy. I wore a jacket, a tie, even a boutonniere. This stood out from all the streetwise comics who were dressed for an armed robbery.

I never used the f-word, and I didn't do sexist or homophobic jokes. In a New York club, that was going to the plate with the batting donut still on.

What was left? How about a bit on the popular new telephone service known as call waiting.

"BEEEP. We're sorry. Someone on the other line is more important that you are."

Or just the truth of my own life.

I used to be a janitor. Now, when I see somebody mopping, I tell him, "Hang in there. You know, I used to be a janitor." Yesterday a guy looked up: "Really? I used to tell jokes in crummy bars."

Job interviews provided the best material of all.

"What's the reason you want to join our firm?"
"Number one? I'm unemployed."
"I see. Do you have any experience?"
"Yes. I've been unemployed many times."

The big club I haunted was Catch a Rising Star. I wasn't rising so much as idling on the tarmac, but inside that circle the balloon might inflate. I would go there Tuesday nights and try to get on, along with other neophytes, and some future icons.

And many were. A young, strange Adam Sandler stopped by. Ditto Chris Rock, not yet sure of his voice. Joy Behar was already cool and in command. Tim McCarver was in the room one night and got a big hand at ringside. Catch was the place to see, and be seen.

Only I couldn't get seen. The idea of auditioning was to "pass" – the club manager gave you his blessing, and you were then part of the ad hoc roster. This might lead to an immediate deal with an agent or some producer, or just more stage time, during which you hoped you weren't going down in flames when Colonel Tom wandered through.

The protocol was, you got there early and tried to get your name on the list. I only managed that once, no matter how promptly I showed up (it wasn't exactly first-come, first-served) and that evening I got bumped for David Brenner.

He dropped in to sleepwalk through some bit he was tuning up, and that was the way things worked. Joy Behar said, "His boots did five minutes and then he went back to his limousine."

In fact, there were so many aspirants lining up on tryout nights they were about to outnumber the audience, and the manager decided to hold auditions on a weekday afternoon.

I got a spot.

With a good set ready, it didn't bother me that the room was comprised of other novice comics, hoping – figuratively or literally – that I would die on stage.

Everyone understood that we weren't there to swap menu ideas.

But I wasn't ready for what happened next. Did I mention that Catch was underneath a dance studio? I hadn't noticed this before at night, maybe they were closed then.

But that afternoon as I heard my name announced and proudly strode up to the mike, what sounded like the entire roster of Rockettes

began tap dancing on the floor above my head.

I wish I were making this up. Try to block out that sound as we continue.

Hi, everybody. I just got laid off – another merger. Soon it'll be just one big company, with two hundred million employees housed inside a giant Walmart. The boss will come out with a bullhorn.

"All right. You hundred million, lunch at noon."

"You other hundred million, 1:30."

"Betty, you watch the phones."

Tap, tap, tap.

Oddly, I didn't pass. If you're appearing with a chorus line, work in front of them, not underneath.

But my routines about the economy kept me going at other clubs. One held a recession-themed contest to find the city's funniest out-of-work resident, and they picked me to emcee.

My big break? It should have been.

The soirée was one morning (a challenging time of day to crack up the public) and the place was packed with TV cameras. Local stations, *Today,* CNN. All about to capture the hilarity. I was ready.

Hi, everybody. Get some coffee? Last time I was up this early wearing a tie, I was pleading not guilty.

On the tube for fundraisers, I wasn't nervous with the big lenses, but I'd never attempted a monologue. I played to the cameras, who don't actually laugh. The media didn't laugh because they thought it was a news event. Everyone else didn't laugh because they thought they weren't supposed to make noise.

That's one I would do over. Later I got a call from someone who'd seen me on CNN. Was that you? Yes! It was me!

But in what they aired a voiceover drowned out whatever it was I was saying. My first national TV appearance came and went without a single syllable. I can only hope that I was a hit with lip-readers.

More mixed results. *The New York Times* must have had a reporter in the audience, because an article quoted one of my lines. Unfortunately, he ran out of room before he could include my name.

Whatever doesn't kill us makes us stronger, said that prankster Fred Nietzsche. Fighting for laughter in my 30s, on stage and off, taught me to stand up for myself, a long time coming.

It was also helpful because I still had that karma of attracting danger. After closing some club, I had to make my way downtown in the small hours on the subway, and thence to the ferry home.

One night I almost didn't make it.

A stop away from mine, a group of what could only be described as *street toughs* came through from the next car and walked down the aisle. We all realized the same thing at the same time.

The car was empty, except for me.

Gulp.

I didn't have time to imagine what carnage I was in for, only long enough to have an inspiration.

I jumped up, ran right at them, and started screaming, "Cigarette? Cigarette?? *Which one of you has a CIGARETTE???*"

A wonderful moment. Their jaws dropped lower than their pants, and they fell over each other scrambling to offer me a smoke before, presumably, I went completely psychotic. Then they couldn't get out of the car fast enough.

I slept well that night.

Calling a bluff and getting crazy to work for me were survival skills. Plus a philosophy that we succeed not because of things, but in spite of them.

All performances have a certain momentum, including the big one that drives our lives. Hanging in there when a line misses or you can't remember the next one – and not running off in a fit of shame and panic – that's how we begin to prevail.

At least that's the theory.

One summer I got picked to emcee downstairs at the Village Gate, a famous place in my East Coast mecca, Greenwich Village. This was a very big deal, a tangible sign I was finally getting somewhere.

Things always went well there. The headliner did a tribute to Bobby Darin without looking or even sounding like him. He just nailed all the songs.

I was experimenting with political humor then, and Bill Clinton was an up-and-coming governor running for president. "Clinton says he wants to do for America what he did for Arkansas. The thing is, the rest of the country already *has* electricity."

The summer shined on, then one night something changed. The place was packed with what appeared to be typical out-of-towners – only I couldn't get anything to work. Not a single giggle, not a nod. They all looked like they were posing for a group picture with some retiring colleague nobody had liked.

This was deflating. Was my nightmare starting again? Bombing *at the Village Gate?* I thought I was past that.

Nursing despair at the bar, I eavesdropped on the group and identified the problem. They knew Bobby Darin, and could finger-snap to the lyrics of "Mack the Knife."

In fact, that was the only English they knew.

Ach du lieber.

The best lesson from those days was to keep focused, to worry about the right stuff. I always call this *The Guy in the Front Row Who's Not Laughing.*

In the real course of human events, he's the jerk who cuts you off in traffic, the impossibly squirrelly boss, the thoughtless relative with a big mouth.

In an audience, he's the guy in your field of vision who lets you know he's not amused, or amusable. Pros learn to block him out, but a beginner will unconsciously start playing to *him*. And in the process, forget everybody else. The laughs get weaker, a joke misses, soon you've lost the room.

Thanks, uh, Larry. Now, let's give it up for a little grandmother who juggles power tools...

You just can't let random distractions take your monorail off track, which is usually accomplished by being the calmest person in the room. There's a Front Row Guy in everybody's life (See *bosses, drivers, people with rashes but no ointment*, above.)

It's natural during life's interpersonal marathons to score yourself, but better when it's like the Olympics. Discount the high score for self-serving agendas and flattery, skip the lowest one for bias and random assailants, and average whatever's left for how you're really doing.

Fight for yourself when you can't rightly avoid duking it out, but learn how to bob and weave, and know when it's time to just cross the street.

That is, if you can spot trouble coming.

I was working a lunchtime show once in New Jersey. The clientele broke up crusty Italian bread as I broke in a routine about my tax problems.

"So the IRS guy asked me (this really happened), 'Can you get the money you owe us from a bank?'

And I said, 'Sure. If I walk in wearing a *nylon* over my face.'"

There were two entities, I pointed out, to which you didn't want to owe money. Those were the Federal Government and John Gotti.

Gotti was "The Dapper Don," the reputed head of the New York-area mob at that time. He claimed to be a plumbing-fixtures salesman, but no one actually believed him.

I thought the set went fine, but when I got off the manager took me aside. She looked white-faced.

Now what?

"Watch those John Gotti jokes," she whispered.

They weren't funny?

"He eats lunch here."

Chapter Seventeen

UP YOUR ORGANIZATION

As a kid my favorite toy was a play set based on the most violent television show of that era, *The Untouchables.* Incorruptible federal agent Eliot Ness chased Al Capone's bootlegging mob around Roaring '20s Chicago in what looked like a Model T Ford, and each week the bodies just kept piling up.

Controversy raged about the influence levied on young viewers, but the play set was just cool. Tiny plastic barrels of illicit hootch, bullet-hole decals for Al's roadster, even a little submachine gun in a miniature violin case.

Historically accurate – and it encouraged us to develop our imaginations.

Kids! Stage your own *Valentine's Day massacre!*

All right, Four Eyes, up against the wall.

Through the eBay time machine we can again locate our lost childhood toys, and I admit to finding this item, but I didn't buy it. The asking price would have settled Capone's tax problems, and covered the co-pay for his venereal disease.

Toys used to be cheaper, even free. I once came upon a discarded car radio antenna and slept with it for a week, although it was no longer connected to a car, or for that matter, a radio. I'd like to think it's still in circulation somewhere. Beachfront property and old radio antennas, they never go down in value.

Television corrupts us all, and I soon coveted the non-free variety of toys advertised there, like "Warriors of the World," little plastic figurines of celebrated combatants, fiercely posed and hastily detailed in what was probably lead-based paint.

Like the chemistry set I made corrosives with, these were *educational* toys. Whose grades would fail to improve with General Longstreet outflanking Erik the Red right there on the dresser?

My father even built a display table for this army. I can't say he didn't try. Which makes the following even weirder than it was at the time. It's a story about work and play, two words used as opposites.

"Work today?"

"Played golf."

"Play tomorrow?"

"Gotta work."

Dig deeper, and these words aren't antonyms, but complements.

People who get the most from playing (basketball, chess, fantasy lacrosse) seem to work at it a little, and those who do their jobs happily and effectively have a playful attitude. They keep their senses of humor, make tasks a game, and don't let the fork lift or photocopier cripple their belief in a higher power.

The ultimate intersection of work and play is known as *retirement*. Some people sweat through their whole lives with no goal in mind but being able some day to play full-time. That's when a few discover they're so bored they have to go find a job.

The relationship between labor and leisure is really snarled inside a workaholic. It takes one to know one, and to father one. Mine had other *–holisms* on his résumé, but work was a bigger addiction than anything you can ingest.

Workaholics have to stay in motion, the same way alcoholics keep their glasses filled without thinking of anything but keeping their glasses filled. The way gluttons eat without tasting.

You can get a lot done, but not with joy. There's too much pride (or shame) at stake. Self-esteem, it's all about the job.

Workaholics dread time off. That shuts down the endorphins from that constant motion, creates time to think – not always welcome – and brings on guilt.

What are you doing *sitting down?* Slacker.

Workaholism is contagious, and inherited. One summer Dad found me playing poker with my buddies and made a big scene. Very embarrassing. Why was I goofing off in the middle of the day? A reasonable question maybe, but he was so *pissed.*

(Note that I said he caught me playing cards. Not shooting out streetlights, tying beer bottles to the neighbor's cat, or wearing a Peek-A-Boo brassiere.)

This was worse. He caught me relaxing.

Never having been a carefree child himself, he thought we should both be on edge.

It's a different view of fun. I still love games, but they can make me nervous. I tried online bridge, anonymously, with three strangers who could be in Vancouver, Bora Bora, or Minsk. I still waited for some message: "Two *clubs?* Are you a *moron?*"

So play is work for some of us, and the line between gets confusing. The first labor-leisure conundrum I can remember was a doozy: toy tools.

Why anyone would want some minuscule pair of pliers or a thumb-length drill, I can't say. But when I was ten or so, I started collecting one company's set, and even made a cardboard tool box to show my father. For some inexplicable reason, he erupted.

Became enraged. Fulminated. Went off.

This was surprising. Unexpected. I was caught off-guard.

Like other memorable outbursts (*The Car Key Caper, The Mystery of the Busboy Job*) this one – *The Toy Tool Tantrum* – had causes I couldn't decode at the time, but seem obvious now.

My Lilliputian screwdrivers would have disturbed him because I wasn't, instead, learning to use his real, professional tools. This threatened his need (I would figure out) to have me validate *his* life by following him into the construction business.

That's where our troubles really started, at ten.

But I was clumsy, and couldn't operate a hammer. I spent one summer trying to drive his bulldozer. I'm also good at docking battleships in fog.

He then reassigned me to painting, which was better because I was alone in some empty house and could crank up the radio.

(Today, whenever I pass some beat-up truck with a sign, "Maloney & Sons," I wonder which boy gave up his dreams to please the old man. I look at the driver and try to guess whether he wanted to be a balloonist or run for mayor.)

Between my indolent card-playing, toy tools, and negative tapes with his own father's voice looping between Dad's ears, I think he started to confuse insecurities about himself with opinions about me. He came out pretty ashamed of both of us.

I once overheard him telling someone I had finally found an occupation: *bum.*

(He meant it to be funny, and that was probably a good line. Humor came to my mind too. I saw myself walking into the room right then with a can of Sterno and a bindle bag on a stick.)

Parents transmit the earliest signals about how to view ourselves. They're our first authority figures, our first bosses. They indicate what to expect from, to *accept* from – and how to handle – those who follow. Along with work/play issues and temper genes, Dad left the message that people in charge *could turn on me at any time.*

I would have preferred cuff links. But what I got was afraid of bosses. Afraid that what they wanted would be impossible to deliver. That their feedback was disinformation, some nutty personal agenda. Praise or criticism, it all sounded like noise.

I had no fun with authorities or played their game well because the rules I learned from had a misprint where the goal line moved but the ball didn't.

Which brings us back to halftime, following that first year in New York City.

I was in a dead-quiet locker room after getting creamed in the first two quarters, as a comic and as an actor/announcer (not to mention as a bearded male model) and the pep talk was straight from Coach Pops.

I went back out, rushed for a couple of bruising yards, got hurt, then called a real audible.

Face to face with a menacing boss on the offensive line, I went berserk and lost my temper.

I told him off *in front of the entire staff.*

As you can imagine, this outrageous outburst got me something I hadn't bargained for.

A promotion, with a corner office.

Even a *couch.*

Maybe we should screen the footage of that upset victory again.

After my early downs as an immigrant entertainer, I saw that I would need a straight job – the famous *day job* – while the klieg lights and I kept looking for each other.

That pattern I'd run before. So why not sign on for the straightest, day-est, entry-level-est job in the entire world of itinerant employment?

I went to work selling Time-Life books.

It was a longshot. Answering an ad, my only credentials were (1) I could operate a telephone, and (2) I was desperate.

I caught a break. That's exactly what they were looking for.

I started on a Monday. We sat in a big room crowded with desks and phones, cold-calling people who'd been foolish enough to cough up their numbers in a moment of weakness. The pitches were all scripted. The prospect said A, you said B. No room for error, and even less to walk around in.

The supervisor, a nice lady with weight-control issues, came in every day toting a bag of snacks. Overcome with guilt, she tried to palm them off on us. She would go from desk to desk, chirping. "Nosh? Nosh?? Who wants a nosh?"

If she had wings you'd have given her the cracker.

This hubbub meant you could barely hear people on the phone, although it usually sounded a lot like *no thanks*, or just a click. The roar was punctuated only by an incongruous sound effect – a little bell.

The idea was, whenever someone got a possible buyer on the line, they were supposed to ring the clapper on their desk, which let the rest of us know that, against all odds, someone actually had a live one on the line and was closing in for the kill.

Ding-a-ling.

This also cued the sweets-laden supervisor to pick up and monitor the conversation. I don't know if the prospects could hear her chewing.

It was a setup I hadn't seen before. A frontier blab school inside an East Coast boiler room, with Tinkerbell hovering in to give the children cookies.

I bailed after a week. I plead failure, boredom, and finally conscience. I heard myself buffaloing some poor little old lady into buying a book on rewiring her house.

End of the first quarter.

Next, I tried working for a messenger service. I wasn't a messenger myself. Those were ruthless, death-defying guys on bikes who whizzed past pedestrians, trying to miss and terrify them at the same time. Messengers were the most dangerous people in New York not already in jail. I just sold their services.

Trudging from office to office in Midtown, I handed out garish, hot-pink brochures with our rates and phone number. The recipient was usually some bored receptionist.

"Good morning. May I see the person in charge of hiring messengers and/or couriers?"

"That's me. Whaddaya want?"

"Great. I wonder if you'd like to try *us* the next time you need a messenger or a courier."

"We already gotta service. I'm busy."

"Great. Can I leave a brochure with you?"

"No."

"Just in case you change your mind?"

"Go away."

"Are you sure? It matches your lipstick."

My boss was, of all things, a retired police lieutenant. I have no idea how he'd made this particular career transition, but the other salesmen did look like felons, so maybe it was a fit.

The central office was across from Studio 54, then in its heyday, although the velvet rope wasn't there at 8 a.m. That didn't stop my colleagues from showing up like party animals between sunrises. Roll call looked like a 12-step meeting let out early.

One bright morning I seemed to be the center of attention. Okay, what now? Amazingly, someone had *kept* one of my handouts and called us when their regular service blew a delivery or maimed a customer or something, and we got their business.

The ex-lieutenant even shook my hand. (My associates were apparently throwing their stuff away and checking into a 24-hour bar to unwind from the stress of the sales meeting.)

Those weeks hawking messengers were spent like a man without a country, with nowhere private to decompress, eat my lunch, or even a predictable bathroom. I finally gravitated to the waiting room at Grand Central Station as my personal headquarters, and used the dubious facilities downstairs.

They'd been busy and elaborate public restrooms during railroading's glorious past, but were now looking like the ones they found under Pompeii.

One afternoon, with only a few fixtures in working order and the growing line of fidgeting patrons far exceeding the available berths, some guy who had been mopping the floor abruptly put down his bucket and assumed the duties of maitre d'.

"You are shitting, sir?"

I beg your pardon?

Politely indicating the urinals and stalls, what would I prefer? His English was pretty good, too. He could conjugate verbs with barely an accent.

"You shit?"

A headwaiter in coveralls. I loved New York.

"That's right, chief. Gimme a table by the window."

It was an interesting place to keep office hours, but I needed something more creative, more stable, more lucrative. That describes either someone who arranges flowers or a crooked accountant, but I became a freelance writer.

Free-lance, of course, dates to those unaffiliated knights of old, hiring out at the drop of a doublet. Today, freelance usually means "unemployed, but I made business cards."

My search netted fish. And paper clips. I was hired to scribe copy for an office supplies catalogue.

I didn't even have to go there much. Which was good, because they were in one of the dingier buildings I've had the pleasure of. If tenants wanted actual windows, they had to pay a little extra.

Some years ago a revolution in desk accessories spawned ergonomic pens and teal pencil cups and clip-on laser pointers. This was before that.

One entire room was crammed with typewriter ribbons, carbon paper, and White-Out. The firm's owner/stockpiler had an unpronounceable last name and looked a lot like my old restaurant friend Mr. Busch. We hit it off immediately.

He hired me to "spice up" the catalogue, revisiting the miracles of Scotch tape, manila folders, and glue.

How? Short sentences. Capitalizing Every Word. Exclamation points!

This style was as breathtaking as Deuteronomy. "A Stapler! That's Easy!! To Use!!!"

You may think this was another tiresome job. You would be wrong. Wrong!

I was developing a new angle to capture the magic of rubber cement when he said we'd taken his catalogue as far into the 20th century as possible.

(It was probably also bittersweet news when the Sistine Chapel was finally done. And I could create art without lying on my back, or getting dressed.)

Which doesn't mean I didn't earn my pay. I was an early work-at-homer, and despite what you hear about the freedom, it's tough to get a break from the grind when your desk is right next to your socks.

My last but most illuminating day job was at one of those firms known as a trade association. (Patience, please. We're coming to the couch.)

Names of industry groups always sound made up. *The American Welding Society. The California Avocado Commission. The Cordage Institute.*

No one knows what they do. That's the point.

They're invisible lobbyists, networkers, affinity groups with authoritative-sounding spokespeople who know how to keep a secret.

Our constituents were America's radio stations – at least the ones who were members, and you'd certainly want to be one, partying (I mean, *training*) at our conventions, getting flashy sales materials, and tapping into a heap of mind-bending statistics.

If, say, someone asked how many female listeners 25-49 knew what "cordage" meant, a guy named Ben could tell you.

This position came with unforgettable coworkers, and I've tried with a few. But I recall Ben fondly. He was a shy, slight, bookish, soft-spoken man who apparently came alive only at *garage sales*.

Grazing every weekend over castoff stuff, especially clothing, he proudly sported his finds at the office, and pointed them out to us on Mondays.

I'm saying Ben *was wearing a dead guy's shoes when you got on the elevator.*

We tried not to look down as he went on about the great deal he got.

Colleagues bring us to organizations. It was the first time I ever saw myself on a flow chart, those complicated diagrams you find most often at firms where things are falling apart.

Fancy designs look pretty lame when the plumbing starts to leak. Hey, isn't this the part where Moe hits Curly with the pipe wrench?

There was plenty of *nyuk, nyuk* at this place too. But it also taught me how big companies work – or spin things when they don't – and how office politicians truly do make or break careers.

All highly instructive, even before the couch.

I reported to a creative director who wanted to be George Bernard Shaw, but found himself squeezing out boilerplate for car dealers instead of literature for the Nobel committee. Clarence was lazy, burned out, and the first person I met whose writing was completely illegible. Not his handwriting, his *typing.*

This was years before anyone could publish their own encyclopedia, and someone had to decipher Clarence's haphazard Smith-Corona keystrokes.

Luckily, the woman at the typesetting machine – an exotic lady from Trinidad and Tobago with a delicious Caribbean accent – was a good guesser.

Clarence and I got into it without delay. He spent most of his day writing plays on company time, goofing off, or rewriting my stuff to look busy.

My patience ran out and I stormed into his office. (People always *storm into* offices. They never storm into a laundry room or den.) I began to shout.

I mean, SHOUT.

Mad, I can get pretty loud. You could hear me from one end of the floor to the other. That's a lot of people.

When I finally cooled down, I couldn't believe my recklessness. A *tantrum?* At *full volume?* In front of *the entire astounded company?*

I figured by the end of the day they'd simply fire me, and tell the woman who sat out by the potted plants to call the police if I ever tried to get back in.

But dig this: they fired *Clarence.*

I hadn't realized they were looking for an excuse. It emerged that everyone knew he was deadwood, and no one testified for the defense when I called him out on the stand.

In fact, they were pretty impressed that I stood up for myself. (It probably helped that we worked in the creative wing of the building. "You know those artistic types, they're *all* screamers.")

But that's the story of how I became an executive, by going berserk in public. I took over Clarence's job, his corner office, and the Caribbean lady with the exotic accent. Quite a haul.

(Did I mention the couch? Ask any white-collar cube farmer. Salary, title, and insurance are all nice, but prestige in an organization is always measured more accurately in square footage and furniture.)

So I moved up and got a closer look inside at an entity that seemed to prosper in spite of itself.

We did have some talent in the building. Adam Buckman would go on to prominence as a savvy media analyst. He and I kept each other laughing. Often about (sometimes during) staff meetings.

I'm convinced two people are the largest group that should ever be assembled, no matter the crisis. Three will argue about what to do, four will argue about whether to do it, and five will argue about when to have the next meeting.

This company had other challenges, like officers whose people skills meant avoiding skilled people.

One senior VP had a policy, it was said, of never hiring anyone smarter than himself. There's some chain-of-command logic to this, but in Vince's case, it tended to limit the gene pool. His division was the Bizarro World version of a MENSA convention.

The president, whom we'll meet, was a brainy guy, but he was replaced by a man who once asked a colleague what the term *third world* meant.

A few rungs below was Chet, the underpaid, overworked buzzsaw who actually kept the place running. There's a Chet at every in-the-black company. Answering his phone, "Purgatory," he cheerfully took crap from everybody, fell on his sword whenever the boss had an anxiety attack, and was somehow able to shave and shower without ever leaving his desk.

Chet was also responsible for the company's worker bees, like Dave, our stereotypical psycho-stalker mailroom guy. Dave disturbed females with his creepy demeanor and inappropriate comments, and Chet finally had to fire him one day after Dave refused to deliver the mail to some administrator unless she let him rub her back.

At the spectrum's other end, the nicest kid there, was our low-key, good-natured, well-mannered office boy, Frank, who never had an unkind word for anyone until he showed up one day with a noseful of angel dust and started yelling at people in the hallway.

This was a little out of character.

But he was apologetic the next day, and we were glad they said he could keep his job if he promised never to do it again, at least not so loud.

This was a lot more cooperative than the attitude anyone ever got from Bill, a man who raised the bar for all disgruntled employees by muttering under his breath after *every* conversation, and finally getting pink-slipped one afternoon for telling a senior vice president who needed something late in the day to shove it.

Bill's defense: Hey, it was already *5:05*.

(After his departure, we had to clean out his office and reconstruct what his actual job had been. There were no clues to be found – except, inexplicably, thirteen bottles of quick-drying shoe polish.)

The most charming man at the firm was well past retirement age, and we were glad he'd stuck around.

The word for Ed was "dapper." He dressed impeccably, described himself as a *raconteur*, and had *MDC* on his business card, which turned out to mean "Member of Diners' Club."

One night, enjoying an expensive cigar (permitted all over then), Ed was accosted by an irate woman: "I can't believe you're smoking that in *here*."

To which he replied, "Madam, just imagine how surprised *I* was to get a whiff of that cheap perfume you've apparently taken a bath in."

Somehow this crew of eccentrics and quixotics kept the boat in the water, and the biggest discovery for me that voyage was seeing the captain in action.

I've always been fascinated with the Presidency (of the United States, not Venezuela or the PTA) because so many people have wanted it, and we know so much about the few who actually got it, and what they did before, during, and after it.

That's a lot of information a person can study about the top job in the world, and I've dipped into some. (I plunge whenever James K. Polk pops up on *Jeopardy!*)

But I never really got the rhythm of power until I worked directly for a number-one guy (that's genderless; number-one *gal* doesn't sound right) and realized that the biggest part of their job is simply hanging on to it.

Leaders cobble a common purpose out of chaos. They juggle competing egos and conflicting agendas, all while watching their backs for oncoming knives.

And they rely on Newton's First Law of Motion: *inertia*. A moving object, or one standing still, will stay that way forever unless something bumps it. People who lead people are all masters of inertia, both ways. They understand bumping.

Our leader was Giles, the mercurial, neurotic, three-piece-suited company president who ran things by keeping everyone a little off-balance. He'd have made a perfect elected official. Which, of course, he was. And he was on the ballot every day.

That isn't to say Giles was *centered.* He had headaches after lunch, his executive VP had them in the morning, and that pretty much shot the whole day for getting anything approved without pain.

Giles also gave the impression he was always just one step away from walking the plank because of some new mutiny brewing on the board of directors.

(I empathize with presidential speechwriters. I ghosted for Commander-in-Chief Giles, who was so afraid of criticism that he grilled me for ten minutes once on whether *let's* needed an apostrophe.)

But Giles was a shrewd man, if a nervous one. Maybe he knew all along that power never lasts. In his case, power made its exit with a punch line.

That rumored *coup d'etat* turned out to be real. The news that Giles was on his way out was dynamite and top-secret, but it spread through the organization like an overturned paint can.

How did we find out so quickly?

Nothing to it. We just read the highly sensitive internal memo Giles sent back to the board pleading for his job. We didn't even have to rifle any desks.

His assistant left it on top of the Xerox machine.

My Laurie knew Giles only by reputation. She would meet my infamous boss at some reception, and might have been apprehensive enough to calm her nerves with a second glass of wine.

At least that's what I think happened.

Because when I introduced the two of them, my polite and proper partner said, "*You're* Giles? Wow. I was expecting someone taller."

Chapter Eighteen

TALKING RADIO

"**G**ood evening, and welcome to another very special edition of our program. They say the biggest celebrities are the ones who don't need a last name. Well, tonight's guest started that trend years ago. Let's say hello to... God."

"Hello, Larry."

"Hello to you, sir. And thanks for coming by on short notice. George Clooney sprained his ankle or something."

"I work in mysterious ways."

"Amen to that. Well, I know our listeners will have a lot of questions tonight, so let's get started. Corpus Christi, Texas, you're first."

"Good evening, Larry. Love your show."

"Thank you."

"God, you're great."

"Thanks again."

"I meant God, Larry."

"Sorry."

"Thanks, Bill. I appreciate it."

"You know my name? You *are* omniscient."

"And they have call screeners."

"Well, I was wondering about that Supreme Court decision saying no official praying before high school football games. Did that tick you off?"

"Not at all."

"But don't you want us praying?"

"Sure. That's why I made it easy. Pray anytime, anywhere you want. But I'd rather you didn't pray over public address systems. You don't pray on this show, do you Larry?"

"God, no."

"Good. I'm pretty busy as it is."

"But what if the football prayer is organized by a student?"

"That 'organizing' thing takes all the individuality out of it, don't you think?"

"Even if it's a cheerleader named Tiffany?"

"I'm afraid so."

"We only want you to watch over our athletes."

"I'm watching. Tell that quarterback to get his degree first. Now go forth, and drink more water."

"Cheyenne, Wyoming. You're talking to God."

"I want to know why those Southern Baptists said women couldn't be pastors. My sister needs a job."

"They said that? Sounds like a wacky rule. You sure they weren't putting you on?"

"Don't think so. They claim it's in the Bible."

"Probably some of that crazy stuff in Revelation. I should have called it quits after Ecclesiastes. You know, 'Turn, Turn, Turn'?"

"My sister loves that one."

"Say hello to her for me.'

"I will. And thanks for all the sunsets."

"Hillsdale, New Jersey. Hello."

"Hi, Larry. I want to ask God about that 'slaves should obey their masters' thing."

"Is *that* one still in there? My bad. It's a typo."

"Are you sure? I saw it on *Law and Order*."

"Happens all the time. And people keep sneaking stuff in, like high school kids giving the finger in their yearbooks. We're going to clean up a lot of this when the new edition comes out. Pictures too."

"Shepherdstown, Kentucky, you're next."

"Okay. Now, right here in *my* Bible, it that says being homosexual is an *abomination*."

"Ouch. Sounds like bad proofreading there."

"Proofreading?"

"What kind of merciful God would make anybody spell 'abomination'?"

"We looked it up at the family values breakfast."

"Exactly. Two thousand years of nearsighted translators, and then everybody thinks they're an apostle. I can't even keep my own commandments straight."

"So where do we turn for divine guidance?"

"I'd go with 'love thy neighbor.' That's still in there, isn't it, Larry? Even the paperbacks?"

"Beats me. I'll have one of our interns check."

"Thanks. I'd rather not edit a stone tablet."

"Kingman, Arizona. You're on the air with God."

"Yeah, I gotta question. This *evolution* thing. I mean, if it took six days to create the whole Earth, then what's all this crap about monkeys?"

"Have you ever heard of the word *allegory*?"

"I don't think so. Is that another warning about homosexuals?"

"Larry, maybe we should take a break."

"Gotcha. And when we come back, we'll say hello to Mary Tyler Moore."

Not too long ago, we loved radio, got mesmerized by TV, and were transported at the movies. Now we *consume media.*

I hate that phrase, not only because it sounds like we're lined up at a trough, lapping. It's just the wrong verb. When we *consume* a gallon of gas or a wheatgrass smoothie, something gets used up, and a transaction occurs. We satisfy our hunger or drive Muffin to field hockey, and we're done.

But consuming a big gulp of media involves nothing so tangible or finite. We never feel full or go anywhere, and there's always more to swallow.

Media was once something to savor, not chug. More apps and Gs are handy, but converting people into electrons for easy portability goes back to the telegraph. The basic idea hasn't changed since breaking news came from some guy on a horse.

What people will want dripping from their spigots has always been much harder to predict than how to keep pumping up the flow. Consider talk radio. Those words conjure up some fascist blowhard, or the smartest guy around. It may the same person.

As a kid I never heard the talky Chicago station my parents had on unless they were reading the list of school closings after a snowfall. But by the time I started washing bakery pans, my ears perked up when a spoken-word feature punctuated the music on my rock stations, *Chickenman* on WCFL and Larry Lujack's bits on WLS. I heard the Cubs on WGN, but whatever else they were blathering on about didn't register. It might have even been news.

When the hits moved to FM, driving cross-country in the middle of the night meant hearing the conversation shows which replaced them on AM.

It was an alien world in more ways than one. Many callers had been abducted by UFOs, which is probably why they had trouble sleeping.

In fact, I didn't see much point in people shooting the shiitakes over the airwaves until I was forced to listen every day, in my restaurant kitchen out in California. Our multinational crew could never agree on a music station, so the radio got left on a phone-in program, "The Feminine Forum," as we did prep.

Women's liberation was a new and controversial idea then, and a show driven by female callers (they hold jobs, they like sex, they even have *opinions*) was unusual and interesting. And a couple dozen females dropping by our workplace via amplitude modulation every day certainly helped pass the time while you were slathering potatoes with lard.

No one knew who would call in next, what they would say, or how we would react. (The comments from a crew of sweaty bilingual cooks were also entertaining, if hard to quote.)

These were regular people too, sounding like someone you knew, and could picture, and would want to.

A decade later I heard Art Rust, Jr., who seemed to have attended every New York sporting event since the Dutch were bowling outdoors. Fans tried to top each other with a question or memory that would make Art's pile of ticket stubs come to life. I called in myself one night with some arcane point about baseball, and was as nervous on hold as I'd ever been in front of my own microphone – hoping Art wouldn't think I was a dope.

It hit me that all listeners really want is to feel respected. Art would never hang up on anybody, so he got plenty of good calls, and never had to.

Talk radio itself is relatively recent. And, like microwave ovens, came from serendipity. They were born after some technician found a candy bar melted in his pocket. Necessity is rarely the mother of invention. Usually it's boredom and an accident.

And so it was one night in 1945, when a disc jockey, playing records as usual, got a call from the bandleader Woody Herman. They spoke off the air until the song ended, then the host had a wild idea.

He put the phone up to his mike and continued the conversation – as far as we know, the very first live, unscripted, impromptu call ever broadcast.

That impulse earned the innocent pioneer a dubious title: Father of Talk Radio. His name, possibly worth noting, was Barry Gray.

Six years later, three media milestones arrived in a single month. I was born a week too early to make it four. That was probably a good thing. My mother said one more labor pain and she'd have jumped out the window.

But we were both around when *I Love Lucy* debuted on October 15, 1951. TV's first nationwide hit is still running, as fresh and funny as that first Monday night because Lucy and Ricky – I mean, Desi – filmed the shenanigans before a live audience, like a play. This was also a new idea.

So the reactions were real (that's Lucy's mom saying *uh, oh* into eternity) and every viewer since has connected with those original, spontaneous laughs. Lucy and Desi knew you couldn't fake it.

Just twelve days before, sports' most enduring sound bite had been captured. Bobby Thomson's "Shot Heard 'Round the World" circulated instantly and permanently as radio caught that convergence of rivalry, upset, and joy on a single pitch.

"...there's a long fly ball and... I do believe... the Giants win the pennant! The Giants win the pennant!... And they're going CRAZY!"

Hear Russ Hodges' call and you're part of the crowd, shocked, elated, jumping to your feet with some fans who took a Wednesday afternoon off and stepped into history.

That October brought a third broadcasting homer and another contest, also covered live.

But in a new way. And for higher stakes than a pennant or an Emmy. The combatants are obscure today compared to Lucy and Bobby, but at the time they were world-famous.

Josephine Baker dazzled Paris by performing in a skirt made of bananas, then by joining the French Resistance. The black girl from St. Louis was the most celebrated African-American entertainer and activist on the globe when she played Broadway that fall and stopped in for dinner at the Stork Club, "New York's New Yorkiest place."

So said Walter Winchell, and he would know. America's omnipotent gossip columnist and grudge-bearing commentator was at his regular table, holding court for stars and publicists, who would stop by to plug their movies and kiss his ashtray.

Winchell saw Baker's party come in and leave, but what transpired between is a matter of dispute. We do know a delay in serving Baker's group was interpreted as a racial snub, and if that was intentional, then the most sophisticated spot in the most sophisticated city in America could act like any Mississippi lunch counter. And that was news.

Baker and Winchell faced off nastily and publicly, two years before *Brown v. Board of Education* and four before Rosa Parks.

Prominent or not, Josephine Baker was an outsider and underdog next to Walter Winchell, who represented the Establishment and the media elite. She was just a woman of color who may have been mistreated. (Who lived in France, and was *pushy.*)

So it started as an uneven match, but then Baker was invited on a radio talk show to tell her side of the story, live and unbridled.

Nothing leveled America's playing field faster.

The whole thing was unprecedented, given the players and that era, in which movies were censored to death, radio scripts were all edited by skittish sponsors, and even news reporting was crippled by the people being reported on.

(Literally. That the last president *couldn't walk* was a little secret kept from the public, with the media's collusion, for 12 years.)

Broadcasting's early regulators thought it should serve the public (don't laugh) but the pile of cash to be made selling Ovaltine quickly turned it into a corporate franchise, no ad-libbing allowed.

When Josephine Baker blasted Walter Winchell live, the tent was being pried open by a rogue host, admitting an aggrieved citizen to plead her own case in her own words, with the world empaneled as an instant jury.

The impact was startling, and irreversible.

Quite a month. Lucy's audience laughing, Bobby's fans cheering, Baker's public demanding the truth. What these breakthroughs had in common were ordinary people who were suddenly visible and taking charge, full participants in what was heard, seen, or known.

People *outside the media.*

Uh oh.

In a twisty postscript, two coincidences wrapped up that fateful fall. The station on the Winchell-Baker hot seat turned out to be WMCA, the same flagship which had aired Thomson's home run.

And the host who put that controversy on the air (and nearly paid with his own career when Winchell retaliated) was the same troublemaker who'd connected the wires in the first place.

Another shout-out to Barry Gray.

I will now make a cameo appearance.

It came three decades later.

Talk radio had become a national juggernaut. (*Juggernaut*, says Merriam-Webster, is British English for "a large, heavy truck.")

Rush Limbaugh wielded as much influence as any elected official. "I'll tell you what to think," he assured his listeners, proudly called Dittoheads. That saved time.

Laura Schlessinger parlayed a physiology Ph. D. into a role as America's Moral Compass. "I don't do debates," she would say, another time-saver.

Six degrees later, I was at a station carrying Rush and Dr. Laura, and we three improbably shared a billboard. They looked confident and prosperous, but the photo of me someone dug up could have been a mug shot. (The guy *swore* that those were somebody else's drugs in his pants. In fact, they were somebody else's pants.)

Talk wasn't just for enlightenment-seeking adults. Young men couldn't turn off the music fast enough when Howard Stern interviewed lesbian strippers.

More degrees. I had an unbilled walk-on in Howard's book *Private Parts.* He mentions almost filling an opening in Chicago, one created by my untimely exit from WXRT. Lasting acclaim may be illusive, but I'm always good for a footnote.

By the time Ronald Reagan left office, I wasn't a Great Communicator, or even an employed one. The latest recession had dried up my other work, and I had to look back seven years to when I last came out of somebody's speakers.

New York had made me ambitious, self-centered, cynical, and desperate. Just like a talk show host.

When I hit the media Land of Oz, the big stations were networks with a *W*: WABC, WCBS, WNBC. It was exciting to walk past those doors, but I knew I wasn't going to get inside anytime soon unless I was delivering pastrami.

WMCA was still around too. The Giants and Stork Club station had crested in the 60s playing Top 40, the first outlet in the country on "I Want to Hold Your Hand." Their jocks, "The Good Guys," wore crewcuts and blazers. It wasn't those clean-cut DJs' fault if New York kids grew up Sharks and Jets anyway, dancin' to the hits with switchblades.

By the 80s WMCA was talk again. Their glory years were long past, just a couple of real shows surviving, others sounding like a sightseer wandered in between the Russian Tea Room and *Cats.*

Always a sucker for a low bar, I figured all they could say was no.

This time, the tape I sent was just me spilling the facts. "Hi! I'm available on short notice if anybody there should happen to, you know, die."

But off it went, with my contact listed as one Michael P. Kessenich.

That sounds like an imaginary friend, but Mike was a very real one. Another surrogate big brother, he was from Milwaukee, my Midwest-transplant *goombah.* Mike told me that if you went outside in New York, you'd better have $50 on you.

Mike was an unapologetic experience seeker. He'd been in advertising, was a lieutenant colonel in the National Guard, ran security for the city's homeless shelters, then signed on for a stint in a comedy duo named Peters & Wright.

We had a blast.

Mike was a great sport, and I wrote a sketch, "Bob the Personal Computer," in which he (as the robotic but oddly lifelike Bob) showed how easy it was to keep track of budgets via the newfangled PC.

Mike was a big guy and bald, and the finale was when he leaned toward the audience and drew a large bar graph – across the top of his head.

This usually brought down the house.

Mike also played my representative when that seemed like a good beard, which is how his name wound up at that radio station, which I'd actually forgotten about until Mike called one day and related a surprising conversation he'd just had.

A voice asked, "Are you Garry Lee Wright's agent?" After verifying it wasn't someone trying to pursue a warrant, Mike conceded he was the man.

The caller turned out to be WMCA's program director. He wanted to know if I could substitute while one of their personalities was away for a week. Eleven years after I'd first said, "ahhh" to the Fayetteville dentist, I was getting a second chance.

This news was being processed when the other headphone dropped. Taking a few days off was their most prominent host, then winding down his long, influential career. It's fair to say I'd heard of him. They wanted me to fill in for Barry Gray.

Uh oh.

My talk debut, in the biggest apple in the basket, would be from a chair usually occupied by the first person who ever told someone, "You're on the air."

Whatever you're thinking, insert it here.

With fantasies, you don't have to prove anything. We're all brave in our daydreams.

But when aspirations become events, the time between getting a new job and having to start it is divided into two parts: celebration and panic.

I had a couple of weeks to get fully nervous. I was coming down with Impostor Syndrome again, that phenomenon in which succeeding people suddenly feel unqualified to be leading their own lives.

The big day came and I was a wreck. Splurging on a cab, I then rode an elevator to a suite of well-worn offices overlooking Midtown. If I bit my fingernails I'd have gone through a whole hand on the way up.

After some nervous news-reading and note-taking, I had nothing to do before the hourglass ran out of sand but pace hallways. Picture a man on a mission, but I was a Cub Scout looking for familiar trees.

How did I get myself into this?

That's a question which bipolars (and others with confidence levels that rise and fall, like tides) ask. I tell people to schedule things when they're up, then don't cancel them when the water recedes.

Most advice is easier in theory than in practice. I could have fled the scene in a *New York second.* (The time elapsing between a stoplight turning green and someone behind you starting to honk.)

But then something out of the ordinary happened. That is, I *saw* something ordinary, but at that time and place it was a vision, like a guardian angel.

With pliers.

I'd stumbled into a room broadcast facilities have called *master control.* They look like Captain Kirk's bridge on the *Enterprise.* Or, in small-town stations, like your demented uncle's crawl space.

But wherever they're found, they all keep tabs on the same thing: whether the expensive equipment is humming along, or about to catch fire.

In that instant I realized every line of work has some system, starting point, shorthand, or OSHA sign that's common to every place that job is done.

They all mean you're *inside.* Find a factory with no time clock or an office without a coffee machine. That's why it's the first thing they show you.

Seeing the same dials in a Manhattan skyscraper I first came upon in rural North Carolina made me realize that I was *supposed* to be in this building.

I located the studio, the red light went on, and not one, but two, capable producers started posting things, sometime competing, on my screen.

Play ball.

A sharp director would end the movie there, fade out over some downloadable song.

But the ones I appear in seem to tack on some moral to complicate the plot. Fortuitous breaks and Forrest Gump angles aside, the only lesson so far was that you can survive a hole in your résumé and still be in the right place at the right time, and nobody's getting on Oprah with that.

However, a short message appeared before the house lights went up.

That first show was a disaster.

Hosting, radio programs or dinner parties, you have to be a quarterback and a referee. I got sacked by everybody. Guests wouldn't take a breath, callers talked over me, and I lost control of the game immediately. I didn't want to offend anybody.

Still worried I'd get in trouble for being myself, that nagging trait from my wonder years was a drawback for someone in the opinion business.

Charlie the PD, in a postmortem meeting, agreed. It looked like the door which opened so abruptly was about to slam. But somehow he gave me a second chance, along with the best piece of advice I ever got from a boss: "Don't hide, reveal."

I went out again the next day, got it through the uprights, and he gave me the rest of the week. I was still in WMCA's rolodex when the station gave up the ghost, so to speak, and was born again, as all-religion.

I don't know if any deities ever called in.

But Charlie's message stuck with me when I faced another audition, years later, in San Antonio.

More unfamiliar turf. All I knew was that salsa went with everything, a large military population lived right nearby, and that many Texans carried concealed weapons only because they were too big to strap on a leg.

Hot news that week was the perennial push to pass a constitutional amendment criminalizing anyone who burned an American flag.

I happen to think that the flag represents our Constitution, and no one can burn that except by rewriting the most perfect document in history to punish a group that wouldn't crowd a motel lobby.

I spent an uneasy night doing laps around the pool, looking up at the stars and wondering if this viewpoint would lead to my premature exit from the Lone Star State, or life.

Next day I said my piece and waited for fallout. You never know what you really believe until you have to defend it.

My first caller was a decorated veteran.

I figured, well, this is it.

Never underestimate yourself, or your audience.

He said that he was inclined to agree with me, like when I compared the amendment – Texas style – to shooting bugs with an elephant gun.

He signed off recommending a good place to eat while I was in town.

It was. I took my daughter.

Chapter Nineteen

BAREFOOT IN PARADISE

Admiralty law rules the high seas and all the slow-maneuvering ships which ply them. It features a concept, the *agony of collision,* which is the time between a crash appearing inevitable and the actual crunching of metal that spills everyone's drink.

There's ample opportunity for agony all around, but hopefully enough warning for passengers, crew, and even the captain to jump overboard, hire a lawyer, or just reflect on some boyhood dream of running a ranch in Montana.

Most pleasure cruises don't *start* with a collision, of course. One generally hears *bon voyage* on a beautiful morning, with sunshine reflecting off turquoise-blue water, seagulls frolicking in the sky, and a grinning steward setting out the first of many delicious buffets. The part with the life preservers is later.

Gurus steer us away from judging events good or bad. They recommend that we experience them, mindfully. But memories still make their way into files marked "cherish forever" or "forget this quick."

And when things begin one way before changing course, the system gets really flummoxed. Mental paperwork scatters everywhere. Along with delight, there's disappointment, even embarrassment.

A was great, but why didn't I see *B* coming?

Our challenge – a big one – is hearing conflicting testimony without swallowing the gavel. Hanging on to pleasant times which preceded calamities.

Thirteen years in New York were capped by a final one, a hundred miles even farther east, a real riches-to-rags Hollywood ending complete with movie stars.

I came as close to celebrity and celebrities as I would ever get, and it cured me of my childhood naïveté about their world and ways. I also worked through some minor character flaws, like being delusional.

That last pleasure cruise, when treats turned into tricks, departed – appropriately – on Halloween. Continuing New York's urban motif, somebody stole our candy.

That evening, as the miniature Butterfingers lay waiting for little goblins to ring our bell, we heard a commotion. Some big kids (that is to say, *a bunch of local hooligans*) had opened our front door, grabbed the sweets, and were now running away.

This was so wrong I proceeded to sprint down the street after them, shouting *You little bastards! Bring back our candy!*

Sometimes you're on the edge without realizing it.

But this heinous crime was just symbolic of a time to move on, and for a much different reason. Laurie had just given birth to our second daughter.

The latest recession had made my own income unreliable, and a family of five needed Dad to find something, somewhere, and promptly. The closest possibility looked like a job – no, an *opportunity* – in The Hamptons.

Being a regional landmark, this location meant not much to a Chicago boy. I was only vaguely aware of what *The Hamptons* was, or were, and would have guessed wrong at exactly where.

For the record, they're a loose collection of towns on the southeastern tip of Long Island. But that bland description is misleading. It's one of the most exclusive spots on the planet. Where, among other things, the rich and renowned hide from those who aren't.

(There's no Midwest equivalent, unless it's a secluded lake in Michigan or Wisconsin, only the cookout is hosted by some Grammy winner, and that guy casting off the pier owns Revlon.)

The Hamptons are unique, and historic. English emigrants came ashore there in the 1600s when Native Long Islanders were already fishing the harbors. Their descendants still live in close-knit enclaves and 200-year-old houses, and the locals all seem to be someone's third cousin. None of them ever got completely comfortable with luminaries and tycoons moving into their neighborhood, but the extra income turned out to be handy.

This idyllic area became an artists' colony, where creators of all stripes and pathologies, from Kurt Vonnegut to John Steinbeck to Joseph Heller, migrated.

Jackson Pollock dripped his paintings in a leafy neighborhood called the Springs, where my family and I also lived, three decades later, before wrapping his car around a tree right down the street.

(Maybe it's a good thing we missed each other.)

Mostly the Hamptons keep thriving as an idea, and a compelling one. Wealthy people have earned the right to live and play in their own exclusive neighborhoods, without the less-well-off around to distract from their privacy and fun. (Except the ones who cater parties and tend the landscaping.)

I hadn't known many rich people before we went out there; my experiences were with the non-rich variety of American. But a third, socially and economically hopeful group was also in residence between the upper crust and those who facilitate their lifestyles. These folks shared a philosophy: wealth is *contagious*.

Or so seemed the idea behind a new radio station which a group of investors planned. With so much disposable income and off-duty bling flashing there (at least in the summer) a sharp operator could just hold out his hat and the doubloons would tumble in. They thought they'd discovered an easy payday.

I knew the money men only by reputation. But they probably had the capital, even on them. Their *fait* was almost *accompli* anyway. The overstuffed staff was already hired, the paneling was up, they had a logo. All they needed was a morning host.

Tempted, intrigued (and increasingly desperate) I still would have passed simply because it was such a leap, relocating all of us to some uncharted destination, even if Alec Baldwin did live there. And I would have declined, except for two little words.

Billy Joel.

The entrepreneurs asking for my services confided that Billy (another East End resident) was one of their investors. A minor partner, but a participant nonetheless. With that implied imprimatur, I just couldn't hear myself saying no. If Billy was in, wasn't that good enough for Garry Lee?

Eastward, ho.

(I eventually met Billy and interviewed him, like the fan I was and am. That he ever knew his name had been dangled to lure people into the morass which followed, I doubt. He'd have been aghast. For all I know, he may have taken a hit himself and had to borrow some cash backstage from Elton John.)

The first leg of our own tour was all applause. We settled into a rented house just as the station was going on the air. Live coverage included Laurie trying to keep the movers from setting furniture on the baby.

The station's ramp-up and grand-opening buzz was intoxicating. The studio faced main street with a big picture window. As congratulations and well-wishes arrived, a dozen bouquets of flowers had accumulated. "We're off to a great start," I noted. "It's starting to look like a Mafia funeral in here."

The New York Times even did an article about the new venture, with plenty of bold-face names, and one ringer.

"The emphasis on news and community programming is what station officials hope will separate WEHM from the rest of East End radio. That and the standup comic they hired as the morning personality. 'Let's have a weather report,' said Garry Lee Wright, a former comedian and talk-show host on WMCA-AM and now the morning man on WEHM. Mr. Wright walked over to a thermometer in the window. 'It's 54 in East Hampton,' he announced. With the station on the air two months, Mr. Wright has been interviewing many townspeople. 'Tomorrow an interview with my barber,' he said.

"Will Mr. Wright's guests and themes change when the rich and famous are in town? 'I'm not doing this show for Kim Basinger,' he said, 'I'm doing this for the people down the street.'

"Actually that is not an exact quotation. Mr. Wright first mentioned Barbra Streisand as the person he was not doing his show for. But when you work at WEHM stars like Ms. Streisand could be listening, 'and I like her,' he said. 'So cross out her name and put in Kim Basinger.' Oops. Not that he doesn't like Ms. Basinger, he added. Ms. Basinger could be listening, too. 'Better put in a dead superstar's name,' he said."

If I sounded intimidated in print, you should have caught me live.

But I did interview some praiseworthy local residents, among them a young Martha Stewart, whom I admire. In our chat, though, she couldn't seem to get off the phone fast enough. Maybe she was nervous. I know I was.

As inventive in public controversies as in her kitchen, Martha took heat on Halloween when a photo shoot concocted by her staff led to a local cemetery. A few townspeople, whose ancestors had been interred there for 300 years, bristled when Martha posed next to some great-great-grand-something's headstone with a spooky pumpkin.

The reflected limelight continued. I even chatted up the sitting Vice President of the United States, the honorable Al Gore.

He was actually standing at the time, as was I, across a rope line on some donor's meticulously groomed lawn at a Democratic fundraiser. (Thinking back, the Secret Service must have approved me, which should make all of us feel a lot safer.)

I couldn't come up with anything really good to ask him, so I tossed out a softball question about the baseball strike. Would he arbitrate?

He looked puzzled for a moment, then said he'd be willing to give it a try.

I'm rarely mistaken for Brian Williams.

Not all stars shine gracefully. On Fourth of July Laurie played my tireless producer, scouring the beach in search of glitterati to put on the air. She approached Chevy Chase, who was rude to her, an offense I bring up every time *National Lampoon's Christmas Vacation* is on TV.

But I got to meet real and gracious East Enders too, like the Baymen, one of the last generations of independent family fishermen, an endangered clan then fighting corporations, government, and time. Their leader (who introduced me as being from "up the island") had the bearing of someone who just stepped out of the Old Testament.

I was honored when they let me into their world one pre-dawn morning, taking me along as they caught squid. The sailor's life probably isn't for me; I got seasick. But you've never tasted calamari like the sweet, tender fruit of the ocean gathered (just as the sun is coming up) by someone in waders whose grandfather harvested the same waters, maybe in the same waders.

The most memorable conversation I had that year was with Edward Albee. Yep, the globe's greatest living playwright happened to have a home there. I tried to sound blasé by asking, as he prepared to get another commendation, if he'd gotten tired of such events. "If they're going to give you an award," he replied, "you might as well show up and accept it."

I never understood humility until that moment. What a line.

A little modesty would have helped me too. But I was getting caught up in my sudden glamor (i.e., the irresistible tsunami of attention after all those lean years in New York) and it went to my head.

I tried too hard to be the star everyone seemed to want, and I'm afraid I came off as arrogant, not the nice guy I play much more convincingly.

But this is hindsight. At the time everything seemed to be made of gold, like they'd promised. I wanted the ride to last forever, so much that I convinced myself it would. Reasonable people predicted differently, but I was drunk at a free bar.

In fact, the investors' lawyer (call him Eddie, the one who had dazzled, courted, and hired me) even urged us to buy a house. This, he said, would ensure our standing in the community, and keep things rolling. We scraped together every nickel we could, and did it. Eddie even handled the real estate deal. The seller seemed to be a friend, more uncanny luck.

Summer begat autumn. Autumn begat winter. But after the in-crowd which ignites the Hamptons' one-season economy high-tailed it back to Manhattan and Malibu, it suddenly became clear that this time each year the small town they left behind ran out of begats.

The jet-setters' amusement park became a sleepy Elks hall. Without summer money, the eastern end of Long Island ceased to be *The Hamptons* and went back to its roots like any other isolated outpost, hunkering down for another Nor'easter, struggling to endure. Inevitably, the radio station began to fail. By Christmas the holly was hitting the fan.

You may know that many December traditions date from pagan observances. Ancient Europeans couldn't quite get their loincloths around the idea that the day gets shorter after the summer solstice, then stretches out again at year's end.

Our yule log might come from those forefathers hedging their bet, gratefully igniting the woodpile to celebrate their relief – and asking the Sun God to please keep coming back.

Even without loincloths, my employers' business model didn't apparently include the concept of "winter." I guess they were indoors then.

But not the station's staff. Soon to be tossed into the snow like ballast from an overloaded icebreaker, they had been fighting with management and each other since the cables got connected. As the snips glinted in the setting sun, *espirit de corps* suffered.

During one tense meeting, a hungover colleague called me an asshole, an indication that the good times might really be over.

The agony of collision began. In January the owners announced they would not be renewing my contract; I was off the air that day. It made local news, and two of my children were into reading age. This was the other side of fame.

Some manager conceded I "had a following," but whoever those hardy souls were couldn't save me or the rest of us. The guy that the investors brought in to get rid of everybody told one host that they "felt real bad."

Laurie and I were getting a little queasy too. Preparing to evacuate, we couldn't sell the house.

Wrong market, wrong everything. Its mortgage kept humming along though, a problem when my income stopped. To top it all off, our desperate financial maneuvering to become homeowners then spawned a huge, unpayable tax bill.

From toasts of the town to bankruptcy, in a year.

Reeling, I turned toward the northeast end of the island, the North Fork, which is what the shoreline does there as it juts away from the Hamptons, like Barbara Bush making a left turn at Barbra Streisand.

But they'd both like the small farms and wineries.

One station, whose owner we'll call Al ("Psycho Al" to staffers) ran a satellite music feed awkwardly interrupted by a truncated local morning show.

This wasn't exactly seamless. More like cutting into a bowling alley's background mix to say that lane four hadn't returned their shoes.

Al hired me to upgrade this production, and I supplanted their current host, a sad-looking man my son said sounded like he was broadcasting from a dark room.

It's never pleasant to push someone aside, but I may have lengthened this guy's life. He'd had a couple of heart attacks and was seen around the station wincing and rubbing his chest. I asked how he enjoyed living and working there.

"Afternoons, I go out in a boat with a bottle of whiskey."

Here's to Vasco da Gama.

Our navigator, Psycho Al, was the most maniacal manic depressive I ever crossed polarities with. He was running two businesses (the funky station and some executive search firm) simultaneously, and both apparently onto a sandbar. Through his open office door everyone could hear him promising the undeliverable one day, and telling them to stick it the next.

This included clients, customers, and of course my long-suffering coworkers, a jittery group of secret and not-so-secret drinkers, the perennially unlucky, and people who just went looking for the ocean one day and found themselves at a place where the road stops.

But I plunged ahead. There were unique local issues (a legally mandated dearth of McDonald's) plus people living real-life dramas. One nail-biting segment let my listeners hear the first-person story of an air-sea rescuer who'd just plucked someone out of Long Island Sound.

But none of this, unfortunately, could rescue my family. Our nut was too big, the station paid too little, and Laurie, holder of an MBA, couldn't find anything in the wilderness to contribute income but a pre-dawn route distributing newspapers.

To wit: The year before, I had been quoted in *The New York Times*. Now my wife was delivering it.

In the early hours (a full one each way from home) there was time to contemplate agony and collisions.

One commute will live in infamy. On the way to Psycho Al's plantation and encounter group, I was running late, out of gas, and had maybe five dollars on me. After the show I was about to miss, I'd need to cash my paycheck to even make it home, the one on which we were defaulting.

And I had to go the bathroom.

Bad.

In a poignant touch, the drive took me past a strawberry field, just like the one where my flying thumbnails had once been worth 10¢ a quart.

In a movie all you'd see would be a fidgeting driver and a speeding car in the middle of nowhere, nothing but strawberries and moonlight. You'd have to know how the plot had evolved to imagine what he was thinking.

This was it:

I've now disgraced my family, lost our money, can't even get to work, and in about five minutes I'M GOING TO WET MY PANTS.

At disheartening times in life, we often hear someone spin a hopeless situation by saying (or even better, *chirping*):

"Things could be worse!"

I use this phrase too. But since that morning I can point to the exact time and place when they were.

I won't spoil the suspense. We gave up on the ill-fated house, stubbornly refused to declare bankruptcy, went back to our Midwestern roots, paid off our debts, and eventually wound up as solvent, solid, property-tax-paying citizens again.

This took 13 years including the citizenship part.

But I'd gotten us into this debacle by losing my perspective, and we got past it the way you survive all upheavals, hanging in there and trying to keep your sense of humor.

The last Eastern Seaboard fundraiser we attended was with the Internal Revenue Service, in the grimmest, most depressing office you've ever seen.

No one knows what they do with our tax money, but I can tell you it's not squandered on decorating.

Barren walls, a metal desk, some functionary who undoubtedly knew that we didn't have any dough, including theirs.

"Thanks for seeing us," I told her, pulling up a plastic chair for Laurie.

"And by the way, I *love* what you've done with this place!"

The absurdity of disasters, even self-inflicted ones, leads to laughter. What else can you do?

After I got canned, the editor of East Hampton's *Independent*, Tom Clavin, asked if I'd like to write something while I was cooling my heels.

So in the same paper where "Wright Off the Air" had been a headline, a feature appeared in the back with the same title and my attempts at English.

The Long Island Press Club, apparently lowering their standards that year, cited the columns (soon dubbed *News Junkie*) for an award in humor.

The certificate still hangs on my wall, a reminder of our year at the top.

And in an appropriate touch, my name was spelled *Gerry*.

But rather than seem ungrateful (I figured if I made any trouble they'd just take it back) I landed a drop of White-Out right in middle of the *e* and framed it.

You can barely tell.

HOLIDAYS AT THE DAILY PLANET
When even the news needs a break

"Excuse me, Mr. White?"

"Yes, Jimmy? What is it?"

"Something strange is going on. No one came to work at the paper today."

"Everyone is off until January. I just came in to use the bathroom."

"I beg your pardon?"

"It's the holiday season. End of the year. We're on a news hiatus."

"A news hiatus? But what if something happens? Who'll report it?"

"It won't. Never does. See, everybody needs a break. All the big newsmakers take off this time of year. Vacationing, partying, sobering up. No one's in any mood for a pushy interview. So they don't do anything, and we don't cover it."

"What about the volatile international situation?"

"Here's your headline: 'War going fine, say top officials.'"

"Run that tomorrow?"

"For the next six weeks."

"What do we put in the rest of the newspaper?"

"The usual holiday stories. We run the same ones every year."

"We do? I never noticed that."

"No one does. End-of-Year Amnesia Syndrome."

"What?"

"Exactly. Something happens to everyone's memory right after Thanksgiving. Maybe it's the L-tryptophan in the turkey. But they never seem to notice when last year's articles pop up again."

"Wait a minute – like, every season we ask some guy at a Christmas tree lot how to keep them fresh, and he says, 'Make a new cut and put it in water.'"

"Bingo. We've run that since World War II and people still hang it up on their refrigerator. Two years ago it even won an honorable mention for investigative reporting."

"And no one ever catches on?"

"Never. Someone ran a picture of Santa wearing an 'I Like Ike' button, but our readers are comatose through New Year's, so no one complained."

"And nothing new actually happens?"

"Nada. We run our annual story about dangerous toys, our annual story about not groping coworkers at company parties, and then our big annual story about holiday safety. 'Don't set fire to your house with frayed Christmas lights!'"

"Does that still happen?"

"Not since 1947."

"Shouldn't we update it?"

"Okay, here's your lead. 'Organic eggnog and botulism are a recipe for holiday stress.'"

"And that's really it for the whole season?"

"We look up when Hanukkah and Kwanzaa are, then it's bring on the BarcaLoungers."

"But what about those shopping surveys? How do we keep them current?"

"Make up the name of some mall. 'Valley River Orchard,' 'Canyon Creek Meadow.' It's always land formation, body of water, plants. Then quote somebody named Betty saying, 'I'm on a budget, but *golly*, it's Christmas!'"

"So there's really nothing that needs doing this time of year?"

"You could write up some weather forecasts."

"Can do, chief! Any particular slant?"

"'Jack Frost will be nipping at our noses.'"

"Got it."

"See you around Valentine's Day."

Chapter Twenty

RIVERS

Laurie and I walked into a restaurant in Louisville one night, right on the Ohio. They gave us a table, but then we waited quite a while before our server finally appeared, weaving and unsteady, as if the place were floating downstream along with the paddlewheelers.

It wasn't. (I glanced out the window just to make sure.) She was also wearing sunglasses, although dusk had long passed and the Texas Hold 'Em finals were elsewhere that year.

To make up for the delay, however, she cheerfully sat down with us (plopped, actually) and launched into a slightly slurred reading of the entire menu, punctuated with odd comments and an occasional giggle. This whetted our appetite for dinner, if not privacy. Could she at least bring us some water?

At this a light bulb went on. Suddenly energized – *"Yes, I can!"* – she jumped up and fairly saluted us.

"I may be hallucinating," said her confident smile, "but I still know what water is!"

Dinner, after she successfully located the kitchen, was also good, and we left her a big tip, figuring she needed it more than we did.

I could add that this was also one of those zany, come-join-the-fun places *(Bring the Whole Gang! Monday, it's Loaded Waitress Night, and Friday is Blindfolded Darts!)* but that wasn't the case.

Aquaria was entertaining, but our intrepid water-bearer was definitely off the menu. Seeing her so gleefully and publicly buzzed also made me wonder how old someone has to be before getting wasted, at work no less, isn't worth the downside.

The backstory I made up for Aquaria was easy to imagine. She'd wanted to be a pediatrician or a ballerina, but found herself in a different reality. Ingesting a couple of somethings was the way she coped, the tool that kept her anger under control.

"Sweetie, could you bring us more tartar sauce?"

"*No*. And drag Miss Piggy away from the buffet before we run out of plates."

The people and the situations we repeat every day reinforce our illusions and armor. But strangers can catch us with our guard down. Someone you'll never meet again may jog your thinking, or put a mirror in your hand.

So it was with me and Aquaria.

On the surface, we didn't have much in common. Underneath I'll bet it was plenty.

Like: I guessed our floating server struggled with some sort of depression. Nine million Americans do, one in four women, according to WikiAnswers, and they probably asked around.

Maybe she also grew up in an offspeed household like mine, or was even another ACOA.

I might have matched her chemical for chemical that summer night, even if was more gently dosed and better at what they call *maintaining*.

I would have had something illicit in my system, plus a few legal drugs prescribed by some medical professional. With both, the first one's usually free.

Aquaria had also, I suspected, either been in therapy or was thought to be a candidate by someone who knew her. I could say that too.

My first visit to a shrink preceded facial hair.

It was in junior high, and I associate the episode with hearing "Guantanamera" on the radio as I slogged through homework about ancient Egyptians. That weekend *Carousel* was on TV. (I never got into musicals. When a burly character throws someone through a window and then breaks into a song, I become disoriented.)

But that wasn't what was going wrong. I recall being terrified, thinking about death, maybe for the first time. I felt a sensation of the Big Bang in reverse. What if the universe *wasn't there at all*, and I were encased in a chunk of rock. Picture that.

Somehow this translated into wanting to die. I can't say if something was amiss in my brain or the household or at school or all three, and the lyrics to "Guantanamera" don't shed any light either.

But I was freaked out enough to tell my mother what I was feeling. She took me to a lady, who looked like my fourth-grade teacher in orthopedic shoes, and we had an uncomfortable chat.

It was a bad spot for a kid in trouble. You need to talk, but don't have the language. And there's no one to share your secrets – certainly not grownups. Even normal teenagers know they can't be trusted.

I came away embarrassed, wishing I hadn't brought any of this up in the first place. The life lesson I would have to unlearn was, if you're feeling suicidal, keep it to yourself. Or you'll wind up in some creepy room with a middle-aged lady and your mother.

Time passed, about fifteen years. I met my second mental health professional on the occasion of an impending marital breakup. Counseling works for some couples, but I couldn't buy into it for us.

"Why are we here? I already admitted I'm a jerk."

"I know, but I need a witness."

The counselor, building her practice and sensing a trifecta, recommended we see her together and also separately. She quickly spotted the obvious.

"Are you depressed?"

"Yes, most of the time."

"Are you taking anything?"

"Name some stuff."

The operative chemical was mostly marijuana, theoretically a *recreational drug*, although the only vacation I looked forward to was a break from the debilitating anxiety and hopelessness that made it impossible to function without some in my system.

"Well, you'll have to quit before you come back."

"If I could quit I wouldn't need to come back."

Luckily, she was able to toss off a quick diagnosis before we parted. I can't remember what, but it probably made the eventual list. She'd known me over two hours, and they have to do a lot of reading.

Thus began the triangle of therapists, therapies, and theories about my psyche which would flow like another river, the mighty Hudson, which I could see from the building in Manhattan where I met my third, and heaviest, headshrinker yet.

It was the 80s. I was battling New York on all fronts. Between standup comedy and radio tragedy, my mental health was such a handicap I began a book, *The Invisible Wheelchair*.

Ironically, the sanity specialist I crossed paths with then was famous himself. He'd written a guide to mood swings, and had introduced lithium salt to America as the miracle drug for manic depression.

Lithium joined New Coke, and they don't call it manic depression anymore because some of us sprouted variations. But in his day this guy was the Hugh Hefner of psychiatry. Too bad you can't cure crazy with furniture, because he had great stuff.

And what an office. I once watched a movie about Mussolini, who palled around with Hitler when he wasn't making those Italian trains run on time. (Later some disgruntled countrymen hanged him up in a picturesque piazza, but this was before that.)

His sanctuary was vast, imposing, big enough for an echo. I thought of that as I sat in Dr. Lithium's own shout-your-troubles-across-the-room space, ten feet away from his aircraft carrier of a desk.

Buongiorno, mi Duce! Canna you hear me?

With no megaphone or charade clues, this looked like a tough meeting. I shouldn't have worried. He was too big a wheel to spend a lot of time with patients. It was meet, greet, plug the book, then pass me on to his colleague-in-training, Dr. Placebo.

Not knowing whether to laugh or sedate me during our interview, Dr. P concluded I had a borderline personality (true; I would read up on them) but also brought back a classic nutty-person diagnosis to explain my show-biz career: *delusions of grandeur.*

You mean, like, Napoleon taking over Europe?

"Right. But today we have medications."

"To get rid of my nagging ambition to succeed?"

"No guarantees, but the prognosis is excellent."

"How soon can I get back to broiling steaks in a plastic hat?"

But I played along, and went on lithium. That was a little tricky. Along with the daily pills, it required weekly blood tests. Not enough in your system, and you'll still want to kill yourself. Too much, and the lithium will do it.

Bottoms up!

I also got my first taste of a legal psychoactive, Imipramine. (Greek for "I swallowed a blender.")

This began 20 years on and off this or that. Antidepressants, antipsychotics, mood stabilizers, tranquilizers, anti-anxiety drugs, and one counterintuitive substance for attention-deficit disorder which, near as I could tell, was speed.

(My first, and last, day on Adderall, I felt myself growing impatient with someone ahead in an ATM line, and had to stop myself from assaulting him.)

Unlike a broken arm, you can't diagnose mental illness with an X-ray – although we may get there soon with brain imaging, so buy some stock – and we're only now explaining how particular additives knit together whatever came untied up there.

This was before that.

The American Psychiatric Association had just declassified homosexuality as a disorder in 1973. Tony Soprano hadn't yet learned that depression is anger turned inward. Prozac was still a punch line.

But drug companies were scrambling to get *their* new products sampled (meaning prescribed; if MDs took the stuff themselves we wouldn't need an FDA) and every doctor I went to for a physical ailment had me try something for my head: see if *this* works.

I was a virtual lab rat. Or just a hungry man at a smörgasbord who doesn't know which herring has the E. coli.

(Now, of course, everyone speaks in shrink, and TV viewers see pharmaceuticals for sleep disorders, cyclothymia, and whatever that guy on *CSI* has.)

The side effects usually outnumber the benefits.

Tryitall® may cause nausea, dizziness, sweating, tics, body odor, bad dreams, your penis may fall off, and dry mouth.

Ask your doctor.

I did, and read about unstable metabolisms until I sounded like one. I researched Seasonal Affective Disorder (I got the light box) and Vagas Nerve Stimulation (I declined to have a wire inserted in my neck) and something called "transcranial magnetic stimulation," a new electroshock idea you might have seen in *One Flew Over the Cuckoo's Nest 2,* right after Jack Nicholson's lobotomy didn't take.

But prescription pills and pot would continue to compete for my bloodstream's attention, the first rarely working, the other sometimes saving me from offing myself, but otherwise being a burden.

It would be years before I sorted all this into digestible bites. That process included the skills of a psychopharmacologist, whose office overlooked another river, the Chicago, and a decade-long stint with a therapist who picked the padlock of my life, and helped me pronounce "psychopharmacologist."

The latter confirmed that marijuana seemed to be a highly effective, if illegal, antidepressant. The former confirmed that some 20 to 30 percent of people with whatever I have, or had, don't respond to psychotropic meds.

Don't let that get around.

The most famous depressive in history makes a curtain call here, along with more serendipity, two Republican presidents, and the biggest river yet.

In 1856, a company with an eye on the future erected the first-ever bridge across the mighty Mississippi, spanning the Father of Waters between Rock Island, Illinois, and Davenport, Iowa.

Just two weeks later, a riverboat got caught up in the current, the boat hit the bridge, an overturned coal stove set the boat on fire, and the flaming boat burned down the bridge. Progress moves slowly.

A lawsuit ensued. Representing the bridge builder was an Illinois attorney named Abraham Lincoln.

His picture is one of two presidents I keep handy. Mr. Lincoln's is right on my desk, a reminder of a great man who was also a good one. His secretaries said he swung between poles, "The Tycoon" and "The Ancient." His friends thought he suffered from what was called *melancholy.* He was probably our funniest president, and easily our saddest.

Sometimes I talk to him late at night if I'm in a scrape, trying to feel his strength and tenacity. (I know, sounds like Nixon, only I'm not drunk or trying to get Henry Kissinger to pray with me.)

The other portrait is of a president I crossed paths with, so to speak, at a radio station near the very spot of that same ill-fated bridge. That area is where we fled – I mean, moved – after our own bridge/stove/fire cruise in the East.

The Quad Cities (Davenport and Bettendorf, Iowa; Rock Island and Moline, Illinois) are quickly spotted on any map. That's where the river makes an unscheduled right turn and runs east to west. I was hired there by WOC, founded by the father of spine-adjusting ("Wonders of Chiropractic") and maybe the first station west of the Mississippi.

Among WOC's early employees was the young Ronald Reagan, like Lincoln another Midwesterner, from nearby Dixon, where you can easily picture him as a teenage lifeguard. Historians now believe he was born with a tan.

Mr. Reagan began as an announcer, one of the early sports broadcasters who, via the technology of the teletype, delivered riveting coverage of baseball games without actually being at them.

He may have even been the man who found himself in a heated contest one day when the wire went down – and described a batter fouling pitches for half an hour before the connection was fixed.

As they say in Little League, "Good eye."

The Quad Cities made me think of growing up in Indiana. Parades with Shriners and their little cars. Diners where regulars meet every morning. Places where locals don't rush to lock their doors at night.

We went rural ourselves, renting a farmhouse some miles away from town in an area out of a Grant Wood painting. Next door was our landlord, who collected antique farm implements, but lived with his wife in a Mediterranean-style house.

(I could imagine the conversation: "Art, if we're going to have a tractor in the driveway, at least I can *pretend* I'm in Italy.")

It was a friendly place. My first week, a listener invited me to hunt morel mushrooms with him. You don't get a lot of that in large urban areas.

Speaking of which, it's just too bad metropolitan types and their Heartland counterparts distrust each other. That's why our politics won't come together. "Drive in *Chicago?* Those people try to *kill you.* And they voted for *Obama.*"

And city folks don't get small-community life. They think it's isolated and myopic. All they remember, driving through some little place at night, is that the only gas station was closed.

These counterpoints made my three years in Iowa interesting.

One incident actually involved filling up the tank, and how you can get caught not doing your job, or doing it.

Mine required punching in by 5:30 a.m. One early morning I needed some gas on the way and stopped where I usually did. But there was some problem with the pump. The petrol was coming out in cups instead of gallons.

About to be publicly late, I watched in frustration as the numbers turned slower than the odometer on a parked car.

I finally made it in, out of breath, and cartooned this as a slice-of-life experience I thought anyone who'd ever been late to work could relate to.

A couple hours later, some salesman accosted me. "Did you actually say that one of our advertisers has a defective gas pump?" The owner was asleep, of course, but – get this – his *mother* was listening.

As punishment for this infraction they made me do a show from the same station. I chatted about windshield wipers and how beef sticks were selling. Signing off, I measured somebody's tire pressure.

The lesson: never assume someone can take a joke, or recognize one. Next time I'll just say shit.

Most location broadcasts were fun, and we did a lot in that small market, where listeners were such good sports that we could drop in on Thanksgiving morning and narrate their kitchen mishaps, trying not to get gravy on the mikes.

Some remotes were dicier. One tested my fear of things that make you dizzy, technically called *illyngophobia,* also known as *trying not to faint.*

(At Disneyland's whirling teacups, I couldn't decide which would have been more embarrassing in front of my daughter – refusing to spin along with her, or losing consciousness mid-whirl and being resuscitated by a paramedic dressed as Sneezy.)

In the Quad Cities, an even more alarming, *portable* ride seemed to show up at all the festivals, and I finally couldn't avoid it.

This contraption was like a crucifix encased in a gyroscope. The victim – I should say, *thrill-seeker* – was strapped in, then the thing was rotated in all directions, hence its name, Zero Gravity Machine. (My choice would have been *Zero Brains Detector.*)

But I had a crowd to entertain! They buckled me in, gave it a spin, I whizzed around, took my bow, exited to the nearest bathroom, and threw up.

Another physical challenge was completing the 7K race known simply as the Bix, named for Bix Beiderbecke, the hard-living cornetist who pioneered Dixieland. The event draws runners from all over, although you couldn't picture Bix himself making it up and down all those hills unless he was rewarded every few blocks with a boilermaker.

Fortunately, the concurrent jazz festival was more up my own straw hat, and I emceed some hot bands. My standup skills were tested between acts.

"One of the candidates said that if Lincoln were alive today, he'd agree with their platform. If Abe heard that, he'd go to a theater and shoot *himself*."

But mostly I steered away from politics on WOC. There was enough from my fellow hosts, Rush Limbaugh and Dr. Laura, and our afternoon guy, with whom I shared an office, inspiring a bit about talk radio.

"Are you *pissed off?* Call me *right now*. The number is *800-P-I-S-S-E-D-O-F-F*."

We were more optimistic in the morning, and booked famous, if veteran, celebrities. Some, it turned out, just before the end of their magical lives.

Buddy Ebsen was a gentleman, charming as his best Jed Clampett, closing with, "Well, *dogies*..."

Tiny Tim will be recognized by Baby Boomers as the ukelele-strumming, falsetto-voiced singer and crazy person married live on the *Tonight Show*, an event rivaling that year's Moon Walk. When he got my name wrong ("Mr. White") I didn't correct him. I was hearing him call Johnny "Mr. Carson."

We even got the first host of *Tonight*, Steve Allen, another person I couldn't believe I was talking to. But he made it an easy interview, laughed at *my* lines, saying, "Thanks for mentioning my book." Which I hadn't yet, the slickest on-air nag ever. You can learn from someone who invented television.

One of our most entertaining guests was the TV *Batman*'s Robin, Burt Ward. My hand floated over the delay button that whole segment.

Burt mostly wanted to talk about how many sexual encounters his fame had spawned, theorizing: "Maybe it was the tights."

We had a good time, and even won an award for Best Morning Radio Show from the River Cities *Reader*. On cue, that's when then fired me.

Or, I should say, *declined to renew my contract.*

There may have been some small savings in doing so, and I wasn't exactly knocking FM stars off the air. Ready to get back to Chicago by then, I placed a good news/bad news call to Laurie's mother.

"Hi, Mom. I got canned again. But I'm finally bringing your daughter home."

The only sour note from that gig in the middle of the Mississippi was the final bleat, when the new owners tried to hold my last check unless I signed an after-the-fact agreement not to criticize them.

I'm not sure what they thought I had on them, and the notion hadn't even occurred to me until they phoned with this demand, via a friend of mine, who sounded embarrassed.

I could picture the conversation.

"Do me a favor, will you hon? Call up Garry Lee and breach his deal."

I was really offended. What's wrong with people?

"The only thing I'll sign is a letter to my lawyer, and then I *will* say something negative."

(It wouldn't have been news. Everyone already suspected he'd capped his own teeth with a kit.)

But I was bluffing. I didn't even have a lawyer.

Bullies are cowards, however, and they blinked.

She called back and said I could pick up my check the next day.

Friends 4–ever!

Cary Grant died in Davenport a few years before we got there, seven weeks from 83.

It was indescribable – sad, wonderful, moving – to introduce Bix bands from the same stage he was about to mount when he became ill.

Obituaries brought up the irony of that urbane, British-accented, world-renowned man passing away in what one called a "burg."

I think Cary would have disagreed. That's why he was there, about to entertain America, and he knew that's where they lived.

Go Haweyes.

For me it was time to cross one last river, if I could get my bloodstream flowing through the locks.

"Doc, this new stuff isn't making any difference, and I can't pee."

"Maybe we should increase the dose. Try these."

"That's the biggest pill I've ever seen."

"I know. Usually we give this one to a bipolar horse."

Chapter Twenty-One

THE SHOW

The Baseball Encyclopedia is a book you can actually read, but it's better suited for putting under a three-year-old's butt at the dinner table, along with bungee cords and a tarp.

Inside are statistics for every player that ever came to bat or pitched an out in the major leagues. Babe Ruth and Cy Young, and Ernie and Fergie and Ronny and Billy, plus guys who had a *cuppa coffee*, then went down to Peoria again.

In the middle are ballplayers like Adolfo Phillips, overlooked now but up from 1964 to 1972, who once hit three home runs in a single game. He had stomach ulcers, took tranquilizers to settle his nerves, and was hit in the head with a pitched ball during spring training in 1969.

Adolfo came to play. About Leo Durocher, who, ironically, managed both my '69 Cubs and birthstone '51 Giants, Adolfo explained, "If Leo say *run*, I *run*. If Leo say *heet*, I *heet*."

Adolfo's English was still better than Leo's. The only printable thing Durocher ever said was "Nice guys finish last." I'm hoping for runner-up.

As did Adolfo. Playing with four Hall-of-Famers, he gets small print. But that also means he was part of something big.

The Cubs, and also the station they played on. WGN led its league in superlatives. The call letters, for "World's Greatest Newspaper," were crazy Colonel McCormick's *Chicago Tribune.* It was among the oldest, where "Amos 'n' Andy" debuted as "Sam 'n' Henry." It reached the heart of the country by day and most of the rest at night.

Even if it was your parents' or grandparents' station. As a youth, hearing Wally Phillips talk back to his commercials was just weird. But by the time Bob Collins and Spike O'Dell were presiding over a share of ears no one will ever match again, it was the only place I wanted to work.

Big jobs are like baseball. There are just thirty major league teams, no more, and nine men without pot bellies on the field at a time. So it was a fantasy for me (or anybody else) to get to the show. A huge longshot mathematically, if not otherwisedly.

But somehow it happened. I thought of Adolfo more than once after they brought me up.

Suddenly, it seemed, but that's not accurate. Years of tapes to successive program directors yielded polite form letters (although anything with that logo was worth keeping) but in motivational-speaker style I persisted, finally getting one on the phone at a needful moment, with a hole in their schedule.

She had me fill in, just like that.

The first night was all slapstick. I was confused by the parking lot's entrance machinery, and a disembodied voice over the speaker asked if I was trying to break in.

The busy, legendary facilities took up the ground floor of Tribune Tower then, like a round-the-clock diner housed inside the Art Institute. But most of the castle was a dark sea of desks and cubicles at night. With directional issues (I exit malls in reverse, noting the pretzel place) a Hansel and Gretel adventure came next, as I got lost from the studio to the men's room.

My life, as they say, flashed before my eyes. This time literally. The Equitable Building next door was where I first wore a tie to work. Downstairs was the Harvey Wallbanger bar. Across Michigan Avenue was the Wrigley, scene of my victory over Bowling Green and the fabulous crayon map.

In fact a sightseer could hit the Billy Goat for a few rounds (whose photos were mostly alive when I first walked in there) then heave something from a passing Wendella boat, and hit my other landmarks without aiming.

Or me. The showcase studio fronting the sidewalk was allegedly bulletproof (I asked; those New York years weren't forgotten) although not rock-proof, as they would discover after I left.

Another hole appeared during the Blackhawks celebrations that *looked* like it might have been from a bullet, but as far as I know, they never found one. Or a puck.

That studio is an exhilarating, intimidating place. Exposed to the world, it symbolized my time in the glare of WGN. I learned to shine, hide, and duck.

My first in-person conversation with the PD would prove to be permanent in its honesty, in my relationship with that administration, and in a taste of the unpredictable which kept me on my toes.

"Thanks for making my dream come true."

"You may not always be here."

Fair enough.

So began a part- (and periodically full-) time job in which I couldn't believe my good fortune, reached new heights in success and paranoia, and alternately waited to get promoted, or fired, for eight years.

My friend Marty says I was a utility infielder who could come off the bench. If true, I'm happy. There will never be a franchise like that again. The first month I drove seven hours to be on the air 45 minutes. I would have done it for five, and for free.

I eventually got to sub in every daypart except weekday morning drive, plus the height of my broadcasting career, a Cubs rain delay.

I know I've lived a charmed media life, even if the trinkets sometimes got detached from the bracelet. But hearing Pat Hughes hand the station off to me one day still seems unbelievable. Maybe for listeners too. Luckily, Cubs fans will put up with anything.

That apparently included *Nick D and Garry Lee*, a loopy shotgun marriage with Nick Digilio which gave late-partying weekenders from Wrigleyville to Australia an alternative to sleep.

Nick was the quickest talent I ever worked with. An effortless vocal mimic, with a stunning recall of every movie, TV show, band, and pop-culture reference known to American adolescents of any age, Nick will always be a funny, angry teenager.

We had nothing important in common except being left-handed and a distaste for Robin Williams. Plus a fifteen-year age gap to shout across.

But somehow it made sense in the middle of the night. Nick was at his best when we faced off over weighty, global issues, like my tropical fish. He contended, persuasively, that anything which got flushed at the end of its life didn't qualify as a pet.

I never had a better time on the radio, even if I was sleep-deprived.

He led me to many laughs, including the funniest hate-mailer I ever didn't correspond with.

From WOC to WGN I apparently carried a listener with me who didn't like Nick, then didn't like me working with Nick, and finally just decided he didn't like me. That settled that.

You take what comes, but this guy had an unusual modus operandi. He typed on one of those funky old Royals or Underwoods with a broken *t* and opaque *o*, so distinctive in their imprints that the Secret Service used to track down nuts that way.

To add even more uniqueness, his odd-size envelopes looked like they'd been pigeonholed in a rolltop desk since before they built the interstates.

That didn't stop him from disguising his identity. First he started changing his name, then his address (and for a while, his *gender*) on the weekly missives. Had I not been paying attention, I'd have thought a lot of enemies were popping up all over the Midwest.

But I was on to him, and just started tossing the stuff away unopened when I went through my mail.

Here's the funny part. Notice that "psychic" and "psycho" come from the same root. He somehow knew I wasn't reading his rants because just started typing them *on the outside of the envelope.*

The media is a conspiracy even to people who don't hear extra voices. The ones who think yours is coming from their radios *only* don't go away easy.

Most of WGN's listeners were saner. Also smart, articulate, and gracious. There were always lots of them out there, ready to call. We didn't have to skip, or bleep, many.

TV also has a delay, of course, in case some Grammy nominee blurts out a twelve-letter word toddlers haven't heard. Our button also got pushed more often with the famous than with their fans.

George Jacobs was Frank Sinatra's long-time valet – read *Mr. S* – and apparently a long-suffering one. How was Ol' Blue Eyes to work for?

"I had to pack a hotplate, man. He made you cook in the fucking *room*."

Um, Andy, did you catch that one in the booth?

Munchkins, improbably, could be even trickier. Among the few (or only) living ones, Jerry Maren came on to talk about fronting the Lollypop Guild in *The Wizard of Oz*. (Jerry also had a run as Little Oscar, as in Meyer, with the Wienermobile.)

I asked if historians had gotten the story right, that the little people who came to Hollywood in '38 were extras by day and wild carousers at night.

"Oh, that's a lot of *bullshit*."

Imagine that voice handing Dorothy a sucker.

Somebody recognized my own voice in line at a hardware store once – as strange as it was cool – but that was just 50,000 watts, and it didn't go to my head. The eleventh station I'd been on, WGN was bigger than all of them combined. Inside I was more of a little person myself, lost in that Emerald City of wizards, with not many testimonials from the busy, nervous men and women behind the curtain.

It was an interesting position, like being a C student at the University of Chicago. Tribune was such a big pond, I could only do my small best to contribute listenership or revenue. I played (badly) on the softball team to meet salespeople, and pitched others to pitch my show to sponsors.

"The problem is," one told me, "I watch TV on Sunday nights."

Understood. My ratings definitely dipped when we were opposite the Super Bowl.

Summers, with Cubs spillover and weekenders driving back from the lake, I was honored with a slice of WGN's seemingly endless cume audience.

Pilots out of O'Hare, surgeons and prosecutors, college professors and steeplejacks. Mothers, waiters, nurses, and cops. All experts about something.

The incredible thing about WGN was, if a story came up in Uruguay, no one had to toss their rolodex for the Assistant Under Secretary of Interviews. Somebody was already calling in from Montevideo.

I would ask, based on jobs or just observations, if what we saw on TV, for example, was off the mark.

A paramedic: "Last week they picked up some guy *with a broken neck*, and just stuffed him into the ambulance like a box from IKEA."

The heaviest talents at the station were the nicest. Bob, Spike, David Kaplan, Dean Richards. I can't believe I was at the same company as Tom Skilling.

The last years of my ride at Tribune coincided with history's quantum-est shift in media habits, the worst recession in my lifetime, and implosions at companies which had seemed indestructible.

After decades on top and in the black, the giants were like my Big T freezer. Nobody wanted to look inside, they couldn't remember what was there or who ordered it, and everything was frozen in place.

The jig finally up, they used a blowtorch. The press knew some of us were out before I did. (Had I missed a last-minute meeting, Laurie's mother would have heard the news from her friend Gussie.) They fired my producer via cellphone on the train.

I'd never really unpacked my suitcase there anyway, but this was still a lot to process, and in a hurry. Keeping a game face with disappointed fans was the hardest. The best take, as usual, came from Laurie.

"Why do you think they got rid of me?"

"Because they could."

If any sliders were mixed with the juicy pitches during my big-league at-bat, the lesson is that nice surprises and the other kind go on simultaneously.

And that very little happens only to you.

A reporter traveling with President Kennedy on Air Force One once asked, "What would happen if this plane crashed?"

JFK: "Your name would be in the newspaper. In very small type."

In January 2008, Tribune Company changed hands for $8.2 billion. Within a year it declared $5.4 billion in red ink, the largest media bankruptcy ever.

And the most flamboyantly newsworthy. By 2010, *The New York Times* was reporting that its Midwest competitor's latest leaders were going too far in shocking the place back into profitability, and had committed the newspaper crime of the century: *smoking cigars in Colonel McCormick's office.*

Eventually things quieted down. My Cubs were adopted by the happiest baseball family since the Wrigleys, Tribune would downsize and reinvent, and LinkedIn's Tribune Alumni Network lists 2,142 members. It's described as a "non-profit collective." (The alumni group, not the current company.)

In fact, the latter never broke stride going broke. Tribune's restructuring-cum-bailout even included bonuses for some of the presiding executives.

"Great bankruptcy, Stan. Here's a golf shirt."

"Thanks. Anything in the pocket?"

"Don't spend it all in one place."

(Creditors later split into two schools on how to slice a nonexistent pie, and one tried to get some of the money back. By then the checks had cleared.)

They'll figure it out. In the meantime, we still get the *Trib* every morning, my wife goes to bed with Mark Suppelsa, and my WGN business card is stapled next to a Japanese pressing of *Rubber Soul.*

My children will write their own stories someday. I always gave them nicknames on the air to guard their privacy – Smiley, Shortee, and Bud – but they were all facing tough personal passages of their own during those public years of mine, not easy for a father to put aside when he goes to work. Those things included something not easily hidden, when my elder daughter was in an accident.

After twenty-one days in an ICU, she added a few more convincing the staff that she knew who the current president was before they'd let her out.

(The details, titled S*leeping Through September*, over whatever name she's using, are hair-raising. But I'll spoil the ending by telling you she made it.)

Her siblings too, and we're all very proud of each other, although they both go by "Smith."

One date my family remembers from those years is unfortunately shared by all Americans. That was September 11, 2001.

I was still asleep that morning, up late with a project the night before. Laurie called and woke me, which was unusual. She said turn on the television.

I saw live what we've all seen too many times since. With the added chill that Laurie had worked in Lower Manhattan when we lived there, not long before. The second plane buzzed a friend's window.

And I may have buried the lead again in not pointing out that Windows on the World – our first spot for tourist drinks in New York, whose bar became our place, where we decided to get married, from where we could see the island where both our daughters were born – was on the North Tower of the World Trade Center.

My last News Junkie piece was unimaginatively called "A Building in New York." It was about shock.

I gave up satire for a while, and the column.

All Americans were in grief, and the only coping mechanism which ever kept me going was gone too.

If my sense of humor seemed to be in the past, that's where I finally had to look to locate it again.

Years of off-and-on standup comedy had yielded not much success, but several hours of material. Eddie Brill, David Letterman's warmup and then-booker, saw a tape I sent him. The verdict: Not bad, only you're too old to put on as a rising newcomer, and too obscure for anything else.

But like they tell method actors, use it.

I decided to mount a show about my generation. In a theater, with scenes and sights and sounds and a groundbreaking audience that wasn't committed to a two-drink minimum before I even showed up.

The working title, "Baby Boomer #14,888,236," turned out to be a math error, but it was a start.

I finally turned fifty
My memory's getting shifty
Seems like yesterday I was hanging out
With Mickey Mouse

Now my hairline is receding
My gums appear to be bleeding
My prostate's the size of a house

It all began with a giant Jell-O box.

And a story in which generations clash, if only in memory. My daughter and I were at a memorabilia-packed diner when she spotted a bumper sticker: "We'll never forgive Jane Fonda."

She asked what that meant. The years of Vietnam and all the bad blood came back to mind, history she wasn't part of. Our lives only go back so far.

So I asked, "What do you *think* it means?"

And she said, "People are still mad about those exercise videos?"

We grew the show over five summers, what they call "opening out of town," which means keeping your mistakes from the public as long as possible.

Premiere night, sort of, was on a New Year's Eve in Kewanee, Illinois. You wouldn't stumble upon it unless you were trying to, but should. Nice people.

I've lived through assassinations
Recessions and inflation
I remember when we all lined up for gas

But now I'm doing yoga, so I never get excited
Like when that bum who runs my mutual fund
Was recently indicted

Trying to translate my times to a younger crowd, we went up to my old Wisconsin college town next, Whitewater, something like getting an honorary degree from the institution you'd been drummed out of. There was even a dean of something in the room.

I used to be a drug-crazed hippie
Now I have a dog named Skippy

I was assembling audiovisual aids by then. Getting a rare 35mm slide of Nixon meeting Elvis – direct from some archivist at the Richard Nixon Library – was like sweet-talking Rose Mary Woods.

I grew up in that Cold War
With the Chinese and the Russians
Now I'm working up the nerve
To try some liposuction

The show continued, cutting and adding, in what was becoming a homecoming tour. Next we played the Quad Cities, in a Moline theater nestled in the woods. The audience enjoyed our surprises. Like when mikes failed, equipment malfunctioned, and in the middle of a scene it started raining wax bananas.

I went on a new diet
When Newsweek said to try it
But then Geraldo's buddies
Did investigative studies

That 'healthy' breakfast food was filled
With saturated fats
And my lunch now causes migraines
In laboratory rats

St. Xavier University, in south Chicago, agreed to a performance in their acoustically perfect space, probably overkill for my latest bit, a pantomime.

I was also tracing the emotional history of my generation's men, never allowed to show weakness. They were proud of it.

"Ma, I got hit by a bus, but I didn't cry!"

"That's great, Johnny. You're just like your dad. He's an idiot too."

Garry Lee Wright was a Baby Boomer closed its truncated run at Chicago's Portage Theater, a 1920s movie palace, exactly what I had in mind trying to picture the show five years before. You got to the dressing room up a ladder, our videos looked like *Gone with the Wind* on the big screen, and I even wore costumes, explaining health care in a gown.

I had a revelation after surgery, watching TV in
my room. A news story about prostitution came on,
and I realized that checking into a hospital and
hiring a hooker involve the exact same dialogue.

Which begins with: "So how much money DO you
have?"

And ends: "All right, take off your pants, and tell
me if this starts to hurt."

Everyone I loved seemed to be in the crew or in the crowd that last weekend, and the encore got hits from people I never even met on YouTube.

We're on the map
We're through taking crap
Nothing fits at the Gap

We enjoy all forms of popular music
But we still can't stand rap

The Baby Boomer show was every man's dream. Employing your family and keeping an eye on them at the same time.

One of my daughters stage-managed and the other ran tech, draftees in what they didn't always get a chance to see, their father at work, and in makeup.

It was apparently illuminating. The younger one, turning 14, had an insight at one performance.

That audience had been particularly appreciative, and particularly senior.

"I finally figured out what you do, Dad."

And?

"You're a rock star for old ladies."

Chapter Twenty-Two

A BRICK BUILDING

Sherlock Holmes taught me to solve mysteries. He worked hard at them, learned from each discovery, and stayed on a case until he cracked it. He dragged along a best friend for company, and told Watson to bring his gun.

Holmes' strategy, he explained, was elementary. To find a solution, just eliminate every possibility that turns out to be impossible. And whatever's left – no matter how *improbable* – must be the answer.

Now, I have a violin recital to attend.

Sherlock looked brilliant explaining what had happened by predicting the future, and vice versa. He knew the evidence would eventually explain itself, and he just told you who did it before anyone else.

We're all sleuths, or need to be. Life offers a riveting series of whodunits and how-do-you-do-its. Mysteries come in three sizes. Figuring out what happened years ago or yesterday, peering into the future (and squinting correctly), and unraveling the present whenever you leave the house.

Be here now (Ram Dass) eloquently ties them all together – focus on the right things at the right time. That also requires being okay with what's past, and being ready, willing, or able, to face what's next.

Prognostication plays with our comfort zones. We can't get enough, and can't wait to blow it off. Everybody knows no one can predict the future. Except meteorologists, economists, fund managers, seismologists, actuaries, bookies, and other people who do it for a living. (What makes people mad is, they still get paid even when they're *wrong*.)

But that's not often enough to shake our faith. They're not magicians, just good at seeing patterns. Their easiest trick all kids know, but adults discard: One, two, and three is almost always followed by "four."

(By the time we learn "extrapolating," the 1,2,3 sequences in our lives seem indecipherable because we're so attached to the next number somehow being 869.)

Insanity, said Einstein, is doing the same thing over and over again and expecting different results.

So righting the future requires a grip on the past. In mine, with many peaks and few regrets, the first mystery was why a dark feeling always seemed to ride along, like some hitchhiker I couldn't get rid of.

Worry, my constant companion, spoiling the fun.

We know what anxiety feels like. But it's as hard to define as happiness; maybe that's its opposite. I finally concluded that butterflies in the belly aren't real emotions, but a side effect of avoiding them.

Nagging thought or full-blown panic attack, anxiety is the mind and body complaining that my priorities are out of whack. FDR, in a wheelchair, said not to get crippled by the fear of fear itself.

That happens when I'm trying to avoid thinking about something while I'm doing something else. This makes me nervous, and incompetent. I didn't get a good cry in, and my socks don't match either.

Despite the ads, no pills can actually cure this.

In fact, I began swallowing less of everything when it seemed to be losing its punch. That was puzzling until I figured out that whatever I'd been trying to treat was losing *its* punch.

This wasn't immediate.

I finally bought into that binary theory of life, where things go one way or another, and fretting doesn't add to your chances after you do your best. This isn't our natural reaction to getting the next good job, grade, parking space, or tattoo removal.

If A happens, everything will be okay.

But if it turns out B, I'M TOTALLY SCREWED.

Resist this approach.

We can plan for and influence, but rarely control, events. Only our reactions to them. I used to wait until later, but now I try to get a jump in advance.

Assume success until otherwise notified.

Staying vertical is also being flexible. (Say leading Buddhists and the *U.S. Army Survival Manual*.) If I can make peace with whatever *might* happen – within reason, no catastrophizing allowed – then I have a crack at a good night's sleep.

Like making money or Hollandaise sauce, this takes practice.

It helps to predict things accurately, of course. Being blindsided drives people to psychics, religious extremism, or infomercials where you send the guy whatever money you have left.

(I could add *Astrology, Enneagrams, and Other Bizarre Belief Systems That Kept Me From Blowing My Brains Out,* but that's another book.)

The horoscopes next to Word Jumble don't speak to me either. And I almost never go into a place with the blinking neon sign:

PALMS READ $5 • BOTH HANDS $7.50

Still, one edition of Trivial Pursuit has a question about the state astrologer of Massachusetts. The answer is: Darrell Martinie, The Cosmic Muffin.

Darrell was a friend, the first openly gay man I got to know, one of those random relationships which change your mind about some things, and your life about others.

His radio reports ("internal weather") were thrust upon me, and I was skeptical. The things he talked about, like full moons and mercury retrograde, would enter the urban-legend-which-may-be-true category, but this was before that.

The Cosmic Muffin thrived on raised eyebrows. Applying algorithms to my birth data (they did it by hand in those days) he spit out my natal chart.

Darrell favored silver cowboy boots, a lunchbox purse, and what he called "whore blond" hair.

He didn't hold back a lot as a soothsayer either.

There wasn't much of, "Jimmy is a creative boy, and will someday be older." Despite having just met me, he came up with specific dates, character traits I thought were hidden, things from my childhood.

In fact: "You have the second-most-difficult chart I've ever seen."

"What's the worst?"

"Mine."

Darrell was the first person to save my life. He did it, ironically, by telling me that there was suicide in my chart.

The genes, the temptations, the triggers.

But it could be *prevented*, if I saw all this coming.

Credence in that sort of thing – which is known as "magical thinking" by mental health professionals – is a symptom of borderline personality disorder.

But the defense would submit that people who are completely gone don't know it. Suspecting I *might* be crazy always brought me back. Some poor soul who thinks he's Jesus doesn't consider: *What if I'm not Jesus? Maybe I'm some guy named Bob.*

If he did the lights would flicker. That's basically my story too, except for not being named Jesus or Bob.

Which brings us to psychotherapy, and to the second man who saved my life. We'll call him Sig.

Different from Dr. Placebo (as food is from gum) Sig had nothing in common with conventional psychiatry but the sweaters and free tea.

He and I started, logically, with my wonder years. That led to my parents, and hence to their drinking. As far as I was prepared to go with a stranger.

Everyone who winds up on a counselor's couch has issues with an authority figure, or all of them. It's not inviting to spill the most intimate beans in an atmosphere that feels like a job interview.

(I never got to read *I'm Okay, You're Okay* but it sounds nice. I'm more familiar with *I'm a Doctor, and Don't You Forget It.*)

Sig broke the ice by violating what must have been some code of professional ethics – he told me he was another adult child of alcoholics, another ACOA. His father used to call him from some bar, ploughed, to drive him home. Sig was maybe 12.

After that I trusted him, and trusted him with my own secrets.

I hung out with Sig, more or less weekly, for ten years. I like to say you're done with therapy when you can remember everything and explain it.

A notecard here reads "burying my parents" but I didn't literally bury either of them. My father actually tried to bury himself when I was about 16, an attempted suicide. I found him.

This wasn't really a recovered memory, but I had to date it by looking up the song that was on the radio as I followed the ambulance to the hospital. It was "Mrs. Robinson" from *The Graduate.*

What you want in a therapist is someone who can drag out your horrible stories without blinking, then somehow come up with the only possible comment that makes you feel better. Here's what Sig said: "Don't take it personally."

Good advice, in many situations.

I also didn't bury my mother, a happier person than my father, especially the last years of her life, although she had come from her own darkness. At the end, her ashes played a typically funny cameo, which I'll relate. First, something not.

My mother was sexually abused, a secret that she apparently told only my sister and me. It disabled her first marriage, unconsummated on the wedding night to someone she always called "a nice guy."

Bobbi would agree that it was also a lifelong issue in her second, to our father.

Which is to say that booze was the least of their problems, or just a reaction to something worse. Their lives might have gone differently with an ear like Sig's to lay their childhood traumas on. But that whole generation was hobbled and programmed. Discouraged from feeling angry, feeling anything. *Keep your problems to yourself. Drinking will help.*

Unlike Sherlock Holmes, I spent many years looking at clues without realizing they were clues. A little story my mother told me, after I'd thought about it as an adult, finally solved the mystery of our parents' parenting in a single paragraph.

She and Dad were traveling somewhere with me as a toddler. They'd left a stuffed animal at some motel or diner, and were well down the road when I howled.

They drove all the way back to get it.

She was giving me a little guilt, but also saying: "Look how hard we tried."

After my own three howlers, I have to respond, "Thanks! Were you *both* nuts?"

It was the story of two well-intentioned people, victimized as children, with no helpful training in what to do with that noisemaking machine the universe had somehow placed in their back seat.

They did their best, I came to conclude. And succeeded more than a little, which is all any of us experimental moms and dads can aim for. This took five decades coming to.

My sister and I have talked about how the damage flowing through some families is like a hot potato. It's passed down and around, with the potential for blisters – but every generation has the opportunity to take some of the heat away.

Bobbi became a teacher, working with at-risk kids. The hot-potato theory is one of the things she tells them if it gets smoky at home.

Then I hope she tells them a funny story, like that one about my mother's ashes.

After she passed away they were with my sister in Texas, I was in Chicago, and there was a delay as we pondered what to do with them, and where.

Her spirit, as it were, seemed to point to Indiana. I finally wound up taking them north in a suitcase, along with my extra shirts and reading material.

This was probably illegal, but we were pressing for time and I don't think my mother would have cared. She would have just duct-taped the package and stowed it with her Noxema.

In any case, the U.S. Transportation Security Administration picked *that particular flight* to search my luggage.

And came upon...

Nana.

At least, that's what I think happened.

Because they left one of those little we-were-here flyers, and the box had been opened – partially, and then resealed in what looked like a hurry.

"Hey, wait a minute! I don't think this is coff–"

My mother would have thought that was a riot. Or does, wherever she is.

My own remains are still intact, thanks to another guy who saved my life, Dr. Deepsea.

We met when I had an ulcer brewing, and we segued from peripheral neuropathy – handy for Hindu fire-walkers, but otherwise inconvenient – to a little blip Dr. Deepsea identified as an aneurysm which had been overlooked by two cardiologists, Dr. Imissedit and Dr. Metoo.

(They did, however, say I had the biggest arteries they'd ever seen. That made me feel pretty virile, like a porn star in some cult movie for surgeons.)

All this was after a series of visits to the hospital when I was still in Iowa. Those included saying farewell to my appendix and several colon polyps, hello to a minor heart attack, and ouch after I smashed up my wrist playing tennis with Laurie (she won).

By the time I got diverticulitis it was becoming a little wearing on my loved ones, and I tried to shield them.

"How'd it go at the doctor?"

"No problem. Let's have dinner."

"What are you in the mood for?"

"How about some broth? All day I've had a taste for clear liquids."

There were also back-and-forth trips to the drugstore when they didn't know what plagued me. So many prescriptions, I finally deciphered the handwriting.

"Dear Mickey: Don't give this germ factory anything that works, or we'll *both* be out of a job."

But Dr. Deepsea referred to patients as people he *took care of.* He was the first person to tell me to think like a survivor. And he even knew how to outsource to people who wouldn't kill you before the fubbadibubbida did.

He changed my mind about doctors. Which was good, because I was about to meet a lot of them.

I spent two pleasant nights at Dr. Apnea's, a Comfort Inn motel room with complimentary wires. I scored 37 out of 40 on her test, a winner, and she set me up with one of those masks that remind you of a jet pilot, only there's no plane.

Then came an authentic miracle. My REM sleep went from four to 25 percent that first night, the snores that disturbed my neighbors and breathing went away, and my lifelong mood swings began to level out.

Other improvements followed. Dr. Dustmite confirmed that my relentless sneezing was a midlife allergy. Dr. Skin removed pre-C blemishes said to have come from a teenage sunburn. Dr. Eyedrops massaged something new called a *retinal occlusion*. (He drew a picture, which floated.)

Anyone who's worn a gown in front of strangers knows that getting through the system alive takes an aggressive attitude combined with a Zen-like detachment.

You learn to ask questions as you hold still, looking over shoulders as they stick things in yours.

"Just relax, and go to your happy place."

"I would, but it's closed on Mondays."

Dr. Eyedrops required the most patience. Dr. Deepsea had told me not to doubt that he knew his stuff, even if he did look like a Teamster.

I beg your pardon?

You know, big, and kind of tough.

Oh. *I'm going blind, and the only man who can save my vision is Jimmy Hoffa.*

The doctor's building had an elevator that opened on an empty hallway, nothing but two lonely plants that looked like they wanted to make a break for it.

The waiting room was so quiet you could hear a pin drop, although nobody would find it after that. We were dilated to the gills. The magazines ranged from a large-print *Reader's Digest* to a copy of *Guns & Ammo.*

(Right, that's what I was thinking.)

But burly Dr. Eyedrops proved to be a pussycat, gentle and skillful, and the de-occluding went fine.

As an added distraction, his assistant dressed like a babe. You don't see many leather jackets in that setting, and hers was hard to miss, even with one retina.

Then Dr. Deepsea phoned me at home one day, which you don't generally get from the medical community unless you owe them money.

It was my aneurysm. When they're small you keep an eye on them, but mine had gotten bigger, and that's when they start to function like a bubble on a radiator hose.

Dr. Stent would do a procedure. He showed me something they would install that looked, I swear, like it came from the plumbing aisle at Home Depot.

As he explained the operation, I drifted into reverie.

"Your sink leaking?"

"Aorta."

"Well, keep the receipt."

A practitioner I came to think of as Dr. Goofy oversaw my pre-op stress test. That's where they slap electrodes on you to run a treadmill and see if anything blows up. The guy had apparently found his niche in this unobserved corner of the hospital, but it was also possible the real doctor was at lunch and he'd just popped in to play around with the equipment.

I thought of a bit I used to do about malpractice, and how the majority of problems are with a small group of repeat offenders.

"Dale! You left a scalpel in Mrs. Delgado's liver! *Again.*"

But my Dr. Stent seemed like a pro, and I wasn't too worried about the operation, even though it was a big one. I told my friend Marty, "I *could* die, but I don't feel like I'm going to."

"That's what I think, too," he said. This was a good thing to agree on, and then we hung up.

June 23nd rolled around. I was awake early and took a shower, knowing I wouldn't get another one too soon. I tried not to look in the mirror, or imagine the large, permanent scar that was about to sprout. No matter how the rest of the day went, my career as an underwear model was probably over.

Repairs were scheduled for 7:30 in the morning, taking three hours. The next thing I knew I was blinking my eyes at a clock that said 4:30.

Dr. Stent had won the game in extra innings, after they returned some blood I'd donated to myself on spec, and a little ride on their ventilator.

I slept through all that, of course, but it must have been dicey for Laurie and daughter number one, who spent the day on Luna bars, fielding calls.

I always want to say to the anesthesiologist, "Thanks for coming by, Doc, and after you put me under, how about giving the missus a little hit too?"

But it turned out okay.

The following weeks were quiet, reflective, and couch-bound. You know you're convalescing when you can recite the Food Network schedule for the next six hours.

Everyone who confronts their own mortality will tell you that death draws the boundaries around life. Yes, it may end on short notice. Worse, it may *not*.

(You don't have to be dying of anything to benefit from this perspective. Will it matter next month? In two years? To my great-grandchildren?)

Happiness, I think, is when the mysteries of your life finally reveal themselves. This takes work, time, humility, luck, and the unshakable confidence that there's actually an answer to be found.

If I've learned anything else about advice, it's that people rarely take it, want it, or even need it. They already know what to do.

Everyone arrives at their own *Wheel of Fortune* moment. Then they either solve the puzzle, or keep buying vowels and watching Vanna turn the letters until time runs out.

The trick is recognizing a destination when you get there. Mine became a brick building.

Near as we know, it was put up about the same time as Wrigley, and even has ivy. My entire family lives there when not elsewhere, a reality series.

But *safe at home* wasn't immediate.

It was my final shot as an impostor. I bought a rehabbing textbook. I plumbed and I painted. I learned to install a ground fault circuit interrupter Just Like Dad.

The girls say my electrician's head lamp looks like I'm going down to the basement to mine coal.

But it also felt like the final step to manhood. For my generation that began with *The Playboy Advisor*, and is winding down with Lou Manfredini.

We should probably end the story here. I'm coming out of seclusion after I fix Shortee's screen, and a new show is called *Surviving Your Own Life.*

But a detour came up before I could put that production, as thespians say, on its feet.

In more ways than one. This time I wasn't dying, I just couldn't walk.

It was the kind of last-minute lesson they sneak in right after you think you already passed the final.

The AAA plumbing patch, in truth, was just too much of a dice roll to qualify as a tutorial.

I got Dr. Stent, but it could have been Dr. Goofy.

My leg case was different. Dating to *I Love Lucy*, whatever they used to pull me out of trouble and Mom left my ankle slightly wonky.

This went unaddressed even after color TV began.

The rest of my frame also got fully out of whack. Chiropractors tossed me around, X-ray readers didn't see anything. Surgeons wanted to install a hip you could make golf clubs from. I had to get a cane.

The mess got worse for decades because I was too busy with my life to solve the underlying puzzles.

I'm pretty sure there's a parable here.

No one volunteers to pay attention. But my eyes were opened and – in an anatomical phenomenon – my legs came to a head with Dr. Foot.

Another survivor, he reminded me to act like one. To meet him halfway, a year of tests, therapy, braces, whittling away at things that wouldn't heal. I tried to crack up his staff between skin grafts.

The last maze brought back a retro classic: *gout.* As in Ben Franklin. What do we do now, leeches?

Enlightenment and a breakdown feel the same way until the end. I learned to trust myself, the future, and occasionally other people.

My friend Reginald drove me to the hospital.

But it was all over in an hour.

After that everything cleared up, like a row of dominoes in reverse.

My friend Reginald, by the way, lives in Uptown, surrounded by neighborhoods where I also lived. Newtown and Boystown and Old Town.

That's where I drove cabs and hawked radio and played guitar. A street away is where I moved after I came back from California, site of the sea-green apartment I slunk back to after getting canned for cooking lobsters improperly in the suburbs.

There's a lot of energy in that spot.

And another restaurant, which is tucked into the storefronts below Reginald's apartment, a Chinese joint, not the kind of elegant Mandarin dining room where I learned to emcee in Manhattan, more like Chop Suey King.

One afternoon I was leaving Reginald's place.

This was before things finally worked out for me, before they'd figured out my not being able to stand on my own two feet, before solving other mysteries with that same theme.

There was some pain that day, a little limping, and then what you call "dizziness."

I began to faint.

Reginald is about half my size, and him trying to hold me up in the middle of Broadway must have looked like a bad slapstick routine, or a brawl.

Either way it wasn't the kind of thing you want to display in daylight. Pedestrians were coming, and a police car was about to cruise by.

Here's what I remember.

With one hand on me, Reginald pointed his other at the Chinese place just as I was going down.

He insists he didn't say this out loud, but I swear I heard him clearly–

"Stay away from the egg foo young."